THEY WENT TO

COLLEGE EARLY

EVALUATION REPORT NUMBER 2

THE FUND FOR THE

ADVANCEMENT OF EDUCATION

655 MADISON AVENUE · NEW YORK 21, N. Y.

THE FUND FOR THE ADVANCEMENT OF EDUCATION is a philanthropic organization established in 1951 by the Ford Foundation to work in the field of formal education.

Its chief activity has been the support of experimental programs which hold promise of advancing education in American schools and colleges. To date the Fund has been granted approximately $57,000,000 by The Ford Foundation.

First printing April 1957

Additional copies of THEY WENT TO COLLEGE EARLY *are available from the offices of The Fund for the Advancement of Education,* 655 *Madison Avenue, New York* 21, *New York*

Library of Congress catalog card number: 57-9381

47068

TALENT, EDUCATION AND DEMOCRACY

A Foreword

There is currently a tremendous upsurge of concern throughout
the country over our future supply of what is variously termed
"high ability manpower," "specialized talent," or "leadership."
Our rapid economic growth and technological advance, coupled
with new opportunities and grave perils we face internationally,
have sharpened our awareness of how heavily this Nation's future progress and security depends upon competent and creative
individuals.

The issue has been dramatized by the shortage of scientists and
engineers, but investigations reveal that this deficiency is merely
part of a general shortage of specialized talent which affects virtually every aspect of society. This over-all shortage results not
from a decline in supply but from a tremendous growth of
demand. A static or declining society would not have the problem,
but in our own dynamic society it must be assumed that the
demand for talent will continue to outstrip the supply. We will
need more of every kind, not merely more nuclear physicists and
engineers, but more first-rate biologists and doctors, teachers and
politicians, economists and ministers, poets and philosophers.

Fortunately there is great opportunity to expand our future
supply of well-developed talent, first, because our youth population has grown tremendously and, second, because we are
presently wasting a vast amount of potential talent. Despite the
great strides made by American education over the last 50 years,
we are still far short of the goal of enabling and encouraging every
young person to develop to his full potential. The resulting waste
of rich human resources is enormous and is deeply rooted in our
educational system, right down to the earliest grades. *We must*

therefore attack the long-run problems of talent supply primarily through our schools and colleges.

The aim, it is important to remember, is to attack the problem, not the schools and colleges. The central issue is not whether these institutions are doing as good a job as they used to do toward developing the abilities of our youth; there is good reason to believe that on the whole they are doing better. The real question is whether they are doing *enough* better, whether they are keeping pace with our mounting needs, and the blunt answer is that they are not.

To do a better job our schools and colleges will need greater support, but they will need also to make many changes in their present methods of operation. The most critical requirement, of course, is to attract into teaching enough of the Nation's finest quality manpower, for it takes talent to produce talent. Of particular concern to this report, however, are those changes in educational procedures which will enable and encourage each individual student to pursue his education with maximum efficiency and effectiveness.

The importance of accommodating the individual differences of young people of similar age is widely recognized, yet many of our conventional academic arrangements inhibit the nurturing of these individual talents and capacities. The reasons are understandable. Over the years we have developed the "grade system" as a convenient administrative device for handling the "traffic management problem" of our schools. Each child begins at age six and moves forward one grade each year until he emerges from high school 12 years later. Then he may march through four years of college, still in step with his chronological peers. This solution to the problem of educational logistics has many administrative advantages, but pressed toward its logical extreme it defeats our efforts to serve the individual capacities of children. At its worst it has become a chronological lock step which in practice, if not in theory, treats students of similar age as if they were all alike

[vi]

instead of all different. The most serious victims—the most handicapped students under this lock step arrangement—turn out to be our ablest youngsters for whom the pace is too slow and the academic diet too thin.

Having developed these arrangements as a matter of convenience, we have proceeded to justify and defend them on high grounds of theory and principle. There are those who argue that it is psychologically unsound and politically undemocratic for one child to proceed faster or to have a richer academic diet than another. Warnings are sounded against the "risks" involved in proposed changes designed to make educational procedures more flexible and more adaptable to the differing needs and abilities of students. To be sure, there are risks in any new ways, until they have been tested. But what is too often ignored is the greatest risk of all—the risk of adhering stubbornly to a clearly imperfect set of practices which are frustrating the development of young talent at a time in history when this nation urgently needs to develop its human resources to the full. A democracy, more than any other system, requires an abundant supply and wide diffusion of talent and leadership if it is to survive and prosper.

Greater attention to the educational needs of the ablest students is an effective way to improve education for all young people. The typical experience of a school or college which sets out to provide better opportunities for its ablest students is to discover far more submerged ability than was suspected and to upgrade the tone and performance of the entire institution.

The Program for Early Admission to College discussed in this report represents one possible approach to making our schools and colleges more flexible and more effective in developing the diversified abilities of young people. It should not, of course, be regarded as the only approach. There are other promising ones and they too must be pursued.

After five years of supporting and observing the Early Admission Program, the board members and officers of The Fund for the Advancement of Education are satisfied that it has produced lessons from which American education can profit. It matters little what the Fund's appraisal is, however; the verdict which counts must be rendered by the practicing educators, the parents, and all others concerned with improving education. It is to help them in reaching this verdict that the present report is offered.

PHILIP H. COOMBS
Secretary and Director of Research
The Fund for the Advancement of Education

CONTENTS

THE EXPERIMENT TO DATE

IN THE FALL of 1951, eleven American colleges and universities opened their doors to 420 freshmen who differed from the average college freshman in two striking respects: they were roughly two years younger and only a few of them had finished high school.

These "Early Admission" students were the pioneers in an experiment financed by The Fund for the Advancement of Education to determine the wisdom and feasibility of allowing carefully selected students of high academic promise to break out of the educational "lock step" and complete their schooling at their own best pace.

THE PROBLEM TO WHICH IT IS ADDRESSED

The experiment was one of a combination of five projects supported by the Fund as part of a broad-scale attack on two closely related weaknesses in the American educational system which tend to impair quality and impose waste. The first is a lack of sufficient flexibility to accommodate the wide differences in ability, interests, and maturity that prevail among young people of similar age. The second is a lack of continuity in the various stages of the educational process, which too often leaves gaps in a student's education or forces him to repeat work he has already done well.

Although these weaknesses occur throughout our educational structure, they are most prominent and perhaps most serious in the four-year period comprising the eleventh through the fourteenth grades, including the troublesome transition from school to college. They affect the education of all students to some extent, but they bear with particular force upon the able student. Too often the able student is prevented by the "lock step" from progressing as far or as fast as his abilities will permit. Too frequently the result is boredom, loss of momentum, and serious waste of time in moving toward intellectual and professional objectives. Many able students, marking time in an unchallenging high school environment, lose interest in education and do not go on to college. Two kinds of waste often occur at the college level. On the one hand, the student from a poor high school frequently must spend most of freshman year closing the gaps in his prior preparation, while the well-prepared student often finds it necessary to repeat in college work that he has already done successfully in high school.

The net effect of these two weaknesses in the American educational system is a waste of what has rightly been called America's most precious resource—the potential talent of its ablest youth.

FIVE ATTACKS ON THE PROBLEM

With these considerations in mind, The Fund for the Advancement of Education has supported a combination of five experiments which have attacked this common problem from different directions.

One of these projects involved a joint effort by several school and college people to seek out the present weaknesses in curricular arrangements for the eleventh through the fourteenth grades and to devise alternative arrangements that would ease the transition from school to college by treating the last two years of secondary school and the first two years of college as a continuous process, conceived as a whole. This study was a joint undertaking by faculty members of three preparatory schools—Andover, Exeter, and Lawrenceville—and three universities which receive many of their students from these schools—Harvard, Yale, and Princeton. It culminated in a challenging report, entitled *General Education in School and College* (Harvard University Press, 1952) which not only pinpointed the weaknesses in the

[2]

current pattern of articulation between school and college, but went on to suggest new curricular arrangements under which an able student could complete the eight conventional years of high school and college in seven years. This report has become a useful source of ideas for curriculum reform at the high school and college level.

A second project, which stemmed in part from the findings of the report mentioned above, has come to be known as the Atlanta Experiment in Articulation and Enrichment in School and College. This is a co-operative enterprise undertaken by four institutions in the Atlanta area—Agnes Scott College, Emory University, Oglethorpe University, and the Westminster Schools. Its purpose is to demonstrate that the able student is capable of absorbing a much more mature program of studies than he usually receives in his last two years of secondary school and his first two years of college. The emphasis is on enrichment, and courses of a more advanced nature than usual are being worked out for each grade level, with a view to planning the four-year sequence as one continuous whole, in which there is steady intellectual growth and no time wasted on repetition. Begun in 1953–54, the program is now in its third year and the first group of students to enter at the eleventh-grade level are now in college. A recent supplemental grant by the Fund has made it possible to include an Atlanta public high school in the experiment and to extend the college phase to the academic year 1960–61.[1]

A third project, begun in 1952, involves the collaboration of the public school system of Portland, Oregon, and faculty members of Reed College in a city-wide program designed to identify exceptionally endowed students early in their academic career and to enrich their educational opportunities. One feature of the Portland project is its broad definition of "giftedness" and its concern not only for exceptional intellectual ability but also for creative talent in art, music, mechanics, writing, dramatics, and

[1] Further information about the Atlanta experiment can be obtained by writing to The President, The Westminster Schools, 3210 Howell Mill Road, N.W., Atlanta, Ga.

leadership. It involves a co-operative arrangement with Reed College in the training of teachers for work with students of exceptional ability, and in providing faculty members to work directly with such students in high school seminars. The main emphasis has been on developing a sound, practical program for gifted children which can be incorporated into the regular curriculum of the school system and supported by the taxpayers of the school district. The results to date indicate that the experiment has amply confirmed the hopes of its founders. Nearly all of the high school students who participated in the program have gone on to college, and report, for example, that their high school seminars, by providing enriched educational fare and by emphasizing independent study, have been of great value in preparing them for the intellectual rigors of college. During the present school year, more than 2,000 gifted students in 21 elementary and high schools are receiving an enriched educational experience under the program. The level of financial support from the Fund has tapered off to the point where the Portland school district is now paying most of the costs out of its regular budget, and will assume the full expense after the current school year.[1]

The fourth project, originally called the School and College Study of Admission with Advanced Standing, has sought to enrich and accelerate general education in the eleventh through the fourteenth grades by providing able students the equivalent of college-grade work in high school, thus enabling them to "leap frog" some of the early work in college. Begun in 1951 as a co-operative venture involving 12 colleges and 12 secondary schools, the program has grown steadily. In 1955, the College Entrance Examination Board assumed responsibility for the program (now known as the Advanced Placement Program), and opened it up to participation by individual students in high schools through-

[1] Further information about the Portland project can be obtained from The Director, Gifted Child Project, Portland Public Schools, 631 Northeast Clackamas Street, Portland 8, Oregon.

[4]

out the country. The examinations are now open to any able high school student, wherever he may be and whether he achieved his knowledge through his own efforts, through tutorial assistance, or by taking special courses. Advanced courses covered by the program are in 12 fields: English Composition, Literature, French, German, Latin, Spanish, American History, European History, Mathematics, Biology, Chemistry, and Physics. In 1956, a total of 1,229 students from 110 secondary schools throughout the country took 2,199 examinations and entered 138 colleges in September. (Nearly half of these students are enrolled at five Eastern colleges—172 at Harvard, 143 at Yale, 89 at Princeton, 60 at Cornell, and 50 at M.I.T.) A recent check of 4,000 high schools by the CEEB indicated that there will be a further increase in the number of candidates for the examinations in the spring of 1957.[1]

The Program for Early Admission to College, with which this report is concerned, represents a somewhat different approach to the problem of saving the able student's time and enriching the quality of his education. It has the same basic aim as the Advanced Placement Program, but it recognizes that many American high schools are not equipped to offer their ablest students college-level work, and that even in high schools that are so equipped, some students who have demonstrated a capacity for college work can profit more by entering college earlier than usual than by remaining in high school.[2]

ORIGIN AND AIMS OF THE EARLY
ADMISSION PROGRAM

The Program for Early Admission to College originated in 1951 as a pre-induction experiment by four universities—Chi-

[1] Further information about the Advanced Placement Program can be obtained from The Director, Advanced Placement Program, College Entrance Examination Board, 425 West 117th Street, New York 27, New York.
[2] A preliminary report entitled *Bridging the Gap Between School and College,* covering four of the projects discussed above, was published in 1953. Copies can be obtained without charge from The Fund for the Advancement of Education.

cago, Columbia, Wisconsin, and Yale—who at that time were concerned about the problems raised for education by the military manpower demands arising out of the conflict in Korea. It then appeared that for an indefinite period ahead the general education of many young men would be interrupted by the requirement of military service at or soon after the age of 18. In the spring of 1951, the four universities requested support for an experiment designed to allow able young men to complete two years of general education in college before being called up for military service. This was to be accomplished by admitting them to college before they had completed high school.

The grant was made, and its announcement immediately evoked widespread interest among other colleges, not simply in trying this approach to the educational problems created by the military draft but in experimenting with the broader idea of accelerating the education of young people who, although they had not yet completed high school, seemed ready, both academically and in terms of personal maturity, to enter college. Accordingly, the program was expanded to include seven other colleges and universities—Fisk, Goucher, Lafayette, Louisville, Oberlin, Shimer, and Utah. A twelfth participant, Morehouse, joined the program in 1952. This expansion, and the subsequent liberalization of the military draft regulations to permit college students with good academic grades to complete college before being drafted, soon broadened the cluster of projects into a large-scale experiment in early admission to college.

As originally conceived, the program was to provide scholarship aid for two groups of Early Admission Scholars during their freshman and sophomore years. In 1951, the participating institutions received grants totaling $2,118,400 for this purpose. Early in 1953, however, additional grants totaling $1,310,645 were made to the participating institutions to enable them to renew the scholarships of the first two groups of Scholars on the basis of need and academic performance and to admit two new but smaller groups of Scholars with partial scholarship assistance.[1] The following table shows the total number of Scholars admitted by the 12 institutions.

NUMBER OF SCHOLARS BY COLLEGE AND YEAR OF ENTRANCE

COLLEGE	1951	1952	1953	1954	TOTAL
CHICAGO	60	54	23	21	158
COLUMBIA	51	46	24	22	143
FISK	28	36	31	27	122
GOUCHER	19	22	15	17	73
LAFAYETTE	30	23	14	0	67
LOUISVILLE	29	29	19	20	97
MOREHOUSE	0	29	28	24	81
OBERLIN	25	29	17	16	87
SHIMER	34	32	29	30	125
UTAH	40	45	38	30	153
WISCONSIN	52	48	13	26	139
YALE	52	47	3	3	105
TOTAL	420	440	254	236	1,350

The first two groups of Scholars—those who entered in 1951 and in 1952—have completed their undergraduate work, so it is

[1] There were three exceptions to the general practice:

Yale admitted only three Scholars in 1953 and in 1954 because it found that the number of qualified applicants for regular admission far exceeded the number that could be accommodated and hence felt it would not be wise to reserve a sizeable number of places for Early Admission Scholars.

The grant to Lafayette provided scholarship aid for the Scholars admitted in 1951, 1952, and 1953. Lafayette admitted a fourth group in 1954, but since these students did not receive financial aid from the Fund they were not counted as Fund Scholars.

Wisconsin, having been unable to fill its 1953 Scholar group, was authorized to give scholarship aid out of the Fund grant to 23 Early Admission students admitted in 1955.

now possible to appraise their four-year college experience, both in terms of their academic performance and in terms of their social and emotional adjustment to college life. This report, therefore, will focus principally on the experience of the first two Scholar groups, but it will also touch upon the experience to date of the two Scholar groups still in college.

HOW THE PROGRAM HAS BEEN EVALUATED

Through the co-operation of the participating colleges and the Educational Testing Service of Princeton, New Jersey, a plan for evaluating the Early Admission Program was worked out in the fall of 1952. Under this plan, the colleges have kept detailed records on the Scholars and have compared their performance with that of a carefully selected group of Comparison students matched with the Scholars on the basis of academic aptitude. In addition, the Scholars themselves have completed questionnaires calling for 34 items of information about their family and school backgrounds, their experience in college, and their plans for the future. The considerable body of data emanating from these two sources has been compiled and analyzed by the Educational Testing Service.

Finally, in preparation for this report, each of the participating colleges reported to the Fund on its own experience under the program, and two independent evaluations were made by well-qualified professional people who had no connection with the Fund or with the experiment. The first was an appraisal of the social and emotional adjustment of the 1951 Scholars, made by a team of trained psychiatrists headed by Dr. Dana Farnsworth, Director of University Health Services at Harvard University, and including as its other members Dr. Daniel H. Funkenstein of the Department of Psychiatry at the Harvard Medical School, and Dr. Bryant Wedge of the Department of Student Health at Yale University. The second was an analysis by Richard Pearson, Associate Director of the College Entrance Examination Board, of essays written just before graduation by 1951 and 1952 Schol-

[8]

ars and Comparison students on their four-year college experiences and their views about early admission.[1]

SUMMARY OF RESULTS TO DATE

Final evaluation of the Early Admission Program will have to wait until the Scholars still in college have graduated, but the results to date clearly indicate that under the proper circumstances early admission to college represents a promising approach to the problem of freeing the able student from the "lock step" and helping him to realize his full potential. That there are risks involved was recognized at the outset of the experiment, but the evidence gathered thus far suggests that these risks are not as great as might be expected and that the rewards to those who succeed can be very great. The results to date can be summarized as follows:

1. Although the program has operated more smoothly at some colleges than at others, all of the participating colleges consider it to have been successful.

2. In a few cases, some of the colleges made mistakes in the selection of their first group of Scholars, and some were overprotective in their handling of the Scholars during the first year of the experiment, but by and large these difficulties were overcome in the selection and handling of subsequent Scholar groups.

3. Academically, all four groups of Scholars have outperformed their classes as a whole and their Comparison students.

4. The rate of failure among the first two groups of Scholars was somewhat higher than that among their Comparison students, but at most of the colleges where comparable data were available it was lower than that among their classmates as a whole. When the reasons for failure were examined, they were found to be no different for the Scholars than for college students in general.

5. The Scholars encountered more initial difficulties in adjust-

[1] Multilithed copies of the Farnsworth and Pearson reports can be obtained from The Fund for the Advancement of Education without cost.

ing to campus life than their older Comparison students, but most of these difficulties were minor and were soon overcome.

6. There is some evidence that in many cases early admission to college freed Scholars from the boredom and frustration of an unchallenging high school environment, gave them new intellectual momentum, and enhanced their social and emotional maturation.

7. Among the first two groups of Scholars who graduated, the proportion planning to go on to graduate school was substantially higher than that among their Comparison students.

8. Although the period of Fund support has ended, 11 of the 12 participating colleges and universities have incorporated the early admission idea into their regular admissions policy. The twelfth, Wisconsin, which has three Scholar groups still to graduate, has not yet taken any action on the matter.

9. In all but a few cases where such data are available, the parents of the Scholars and the principals of the high schools from which they came have expressed themselves as favorably disposed toward the results of the experiment.

10. The evidence gathered thus far clearly suggests that high academic aptitude and the ability to handle the responsibilities of college life are the *sine qua non* of early admission, and that colleges should not be overprotective in the handling of early admission students.

THE COLLEGES, THE SCHOLARS
AND THE COMPARISON STUDENTS

THE "LABORATORY" in which the Early Admission experiment has been conducted consists of a diverse group of institutions of higher learning. They range in size from a large university such as Wisconsin (registration: 17,800), where the Scholars represented only a tiny fraction of each entering class, down to the small college of Shimer, where the student body numbers less than 150 and the Scholars were almost as numerous as their classmates. Three of the institutions—Chicago, Louisville, and Shimer—had done considerable previous experimenting with the admission of young students who had not finished high school. For the remaining nine institutions, a policy of early admission was new.

One of the participating colleges—Goucher—is restricted to women, and four—Columbia, Lafayette, Morehouse, and Yale—are restricted to men. The rest are co-educational. Two institutions—Fisk and Morehouse—have traditionally been attended by Negro students. As for control, two of the largest universities—Wisconsin and Utah—are state-operated, and another—Louisville—is municipal, while the remaining nine institutions are privately supported.

While this diversity among the participating institutions has not simplified the task of over-all interpretation of results, it has meant that the Early Admission experiment has been conducted under conditions fairly representative of American higher education as a whole.

[11]

HOW THE SCHOLARS WERE CHOSEN

The students who were awarded Fund scholarships under the program were not selected by the Fund itself, but by the individual colleges and universities. In general, each institution employed its own usual procedures in admitting Scholars, but some used special recruiting efforts and screened candidates for Early Admission more carefully than candidates for regular admission.

The Scholars were selected above all for their high academic promise. Admissions officers based their judgment of this on the applicants' high school records and their scores on scholastic aptitude tests, coupled in most cases with achievement tests. Except in the case of Shimer, no applicant was accepted unless his aptitude score was higher than the customary minimum for entering students. Shimer tried an experimental procedure of admitting Scholars with a wide range of aptitudes, including some of average and below-average capacity.

The choice of Scholars was not guided solely by the consideration of high scholastic aptitude. Admissions officers generally attempted a more careful appraisal of the applicants' social and emotional maturity than is customary with ordinary applicants, in recognition of the fact that not every young high school student of unusual intellectual endowment is ready to handle the greater freedom of college wisely. Many institutions insisted on personal interviews with the Scholar candidates. All relied heavily on the judgments of high school principals where such judgments were available. One college found the students' application letters revealing. Another requested and studied autobiographical sketches.

In cases where the academic promise and emotional maturity of candidates were considered roughly equal, the choice was influenced by other factors, some quite unrelated to the intent of the program itself but important to the institution. Most of the colleges, for example, sought greater geographical and socioeconomic diversity than usually exists among their entering fresh-

[12]

men. Most institutions also favored the candidate of greater financial need. Most favored the public high school student over the private preparatory school student. A few colleges, seeking to avoid selecting scholars who would be "conspicuous oddities" on their campuses, favored candidates who looked older than their age.

The selection of the pioneer group of 1951 Scholars was made under a dual handicap which was not present in subsequent years. To begin with, the original grants were made in the late spring and early summer of 1951, which allowed the participating institutions much less time for selecting the Scholars than they were accustomed to have for selecting entering freshmen. At Yale, for example, the personal interview is a significant aspect of admission policy, and more than 80 per cent of all candidates for admission are interviewed by alumni or members of the admissions office. But in the case of the 1951 Scholars, it was possible to interview only a handful of the applicants. One result of this was a relatively heavy loss of Scholars during the first year because of adjustment difficulties. Several other colleges noted in their reports to the Fund that they too had less time than they would have liked in selecting their first group of Scholars.

A second factor which made selection of the 1951 Scholars more difficult than the selection of subsequent groups was the inexperience of most of the colleges in recruiting such students and in gauging their social and emotional readiness for college. This is far more difficult to measure than academic readiness, and techniques of appraisal had to be learned.

In general, subsequent groups of Scholars were much more skillfully chosen than the 1951 group. The colleges and universities, benefiting from experience, refined their techniques considerably as the program continued.

CHARACTERISTICS OF THE SCHOLARS

Not long after the program was launched, the campus humor magazine at one college poked fun at the early admission experiment by running an interview with a mythical Scholar named "Percival Suckthumb, aged 9, senior major in atomic physics." The college observed in its report to the Fund that the authorship was shrouded in mystery but that the article may well have been written by one of the Scholars. The case seems worth citing, not as an indication of the general collegiate attitude, but because the caricature is perhaps not far removed from the concept of the Scholars held by some people who have had no first-hand experience with them.

What were the Fund Scholars really like? From what kind of families, high schools, and community backgrounds did they come? While it is as impossible to produce a truly typical Scholar as it is to produce a truly typical college student, Chart I (pages 16 and 17) affords as clear a composite portrait of the Fund Scholar as it is possible to present. It is based on statistics for the four combined Scholar groups.

As the chart indicates, the Scholars were not "infant prodigies" or "baby geniuses," but merely students who happened to be relatively younger and relatively more promising intellectually than ordinary students. Most of them were 16 years old or younger, and only a small minority had completed 12 years of schooling before entering college. The majority came from large cities or suburbs, but roughly 10 per cent came from small towns and another 10 per cent from rural areas. By and large, they were the products of public schools, and most of them were from middle-income families whose breadwinner was either in business or one of the professions.

THE COMPARISON STUDENTS

Because the Scholars as a whole were considerably above average in scholastic aptitude, it was important to compare their progress in college not only with that of their classmates in general but also with that of a group of carefully selected "matching" students of comparable aptitude. This was done at all of the colleges except Shimer, where, as has already been pointed out, the Scholars had a wide range of aptitude scores and were almost as numerous as their classmates.

These Comparison students differed from the Scholars in two important respects—they were about two years older, and they had completed high school. They were matched with the Scholars on the basis of aptitude scores. Some of the colleges used the College Board Scholastic Aptitude test for this purpose, others used the American Council on Education Psychological Examination, and still others used these "yardsticks" in combination. In general, the Scholars and Comparisons were about equal on these various measures of aptitude; where there were small differences in mean scores, they tended to be in favor of the Scholars.

Some of the colleges made an effort to apply other factors—such as family background, type and location of home community, and amount of scholarship aid, in doing the matching. Most of the Comparison students were aware of their role in the experiment, and some displayed a lively interest in it.

HOW THE COLLEGES HANDLED THE SCHOLARS

Most of the colleges and universities participating in the program have made it a point to give Scholars the same academic treatment as other entering freshmen. The heavy emphasis in the freshman and sophomore years has been on a liberal or general education. In most institutions—with Goucher and Oberlin as notable exceptions—the Scholars, along with other entering students, have been allowed relatively little choice as to curriculum in the first two years. Typically, they have entered prescribed courses in the social sciences, natural sciences, mathematics, and humanities, often with a foreign language as well.

In six institutions—Columbia, Chicago, Goucher, Louisville, Oberlin, and Shimer—academic arrangements for the Scholars have not differed in any respect from those for other students. The same has been generally true at Lafayette, although engineering Scholars at this college have been given a special in-

CHART I

WHAT THE SCHOLARS WERE LIKE*

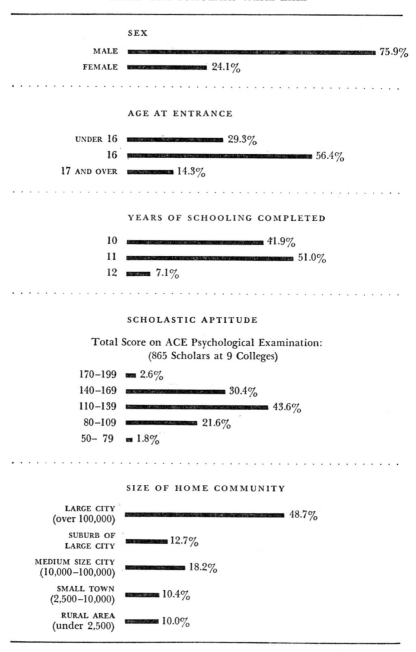

SEX

MALE 75.9%

FEMALE 24.1%

AGE AT ENTRANCE

UNDER 16 29.3%

16 56.4%

17 AND OVER 14.3%

YEARS OF SCHOOLING COMPLETED

10 41.9%

11 51.0%

12 7.1%

SCHOLASTIC APTITUDE

Total Score on ACE Psychological Examination:
(865 Scholars at 9 Colleges)

170–199 2.6%

140–169 30.4%

110–139 43.6%

80–109 21.6%

50– 79 1.8%

SIZE OF HOME COMMUNITY

LARGE CITY
(over 100,000) 48.7%

SUBURB OF
LARGE CITY 12.7%

MEDIUM SIZE CITY
(10,000–100,000) 18.2%

SMALL TOWN
(2,500–10,000) 10.4%

RURAL AREA
(under 2,500) 10.0%

CHART I

WHAT THE SCHOLARS WERE LIKE*

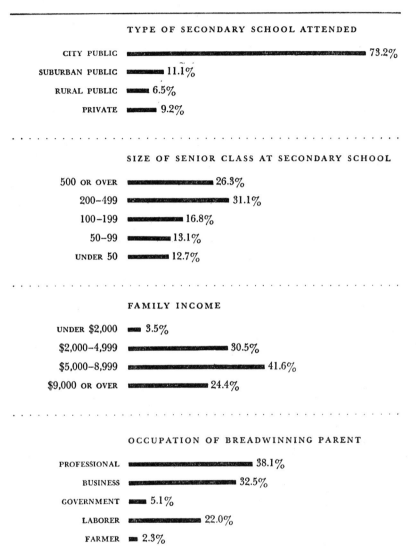

TYPE OF SECONDARY SCHOOL ATTENDED

CITY PUBLIC — 73.2%
SUBURBAN PUBLIC — 11.1%
RURAL PUBLIC — 6.5%
PRIVATE — 9.2%

SIZE OF SENIOR CLASS AT SECONDARY SCHOOL

500 OR OVER — 26.3%
200–499 — 31.1%
100–199 — 16.8%
50–99 — 13.1%
UNDER 50 — 12.7%

FAMILY INCOME

UNDER $2,000 — 3.5%
$2,000–4,999 — 30.5%
$5,000–8,999 — 41.6%
$9,000 OR OVER — 24.4%

OCCUPATION OF BREADWINNING PARENT

PROFESSIONAL — 38.1%
BUSINESS — 32.5%
GOVERNMENT — 5.1%
LABORER — 22.0%
FARMER — 2.3%

* Percentages exclude Scholars for whom no data were available.

tegrated course in Mathematics and Physics designed in part to compensate for what they had missed in high school.

At some institutions special academic arrangements were organized for the Scholars in order to provide them with a richer educational experience than the regular curriculum allowed. At Yale, for example, the Scholars were required to enter a program of Directed Studies—which had begun as an experiment in 1945—along with roughly two-thirds as many regular students.

A similar policy was set at Wisconsin as the program was launched. Three-fifths of the Scholars were required to enter an integrated Liberal Studies program, and the others were assigned more work in humanities and social studies than regular students. Special handling also occurred at Utah. New courses in history, philosophy, and mathematics were organized for the Scholars at this university and special advanced sections of other courses were reserved exclusively for them.

Only Yale continued these special arrangements unchanged. At Wisconsin and Utah, experience led to their abandonment or modification. This change occurred partly as a result of strong Scholar protests against being set apart from other students.

Fisk was the only institution to segregate its Scholars completely in terms of academic arrangements, but this policy too has been revised. When the program began, all Scholars (and only Scholars) were enrolled in a newly established "Basic College" with an entirely separate faculty. This new "College" had been planned for some time, and was put into operation a year ahead of schedule, with a richer curriculum and higher standards than the regular college. After the first year several of its courses were opened to all freshmen.

While most of the participating institutions offer at least a limited opportunity for the academic acceleration of their students, few have genuine "acceleration" systems. Chicago and Shimer, the notable exceptions, have a highly flexible policy. They have for many years not only admitted students early, but also permitted wide differences in their rate of progress through college. The other colleges and universities maintain curricula organized on the conventional premise that virtually every student should spend four years acquiring a minimum quota of course credits to earn a bachelor's degree.

In the non-academic aspects of college life, the majority of the colleges have treated the Scholars exactly like other students. They have permitted and encouraged the Scholars to participate in extra-curricular activities. On most campuses, the Scholars have been subject to the same regulations as other freshmen, though because of their age they have been generally discouraged or prohibited from joining fraternities during the freshman or sophomore year.

There were some colleges, however, where special social arrangements were made for the Scholars during the first year of the experiment. At Fisk, for example, it was decided to assign the first group of Scholars to separate dormitories in which they were required to take their evening meal apart from other students, and their social activities were strictly supervised. At Yale, the 1951 Scholars were assigned to dormitories as a group, and other special provisions were made to set them apart from the student body as a whole. At Columbia, Oberlin, and Goucher, the 1951 Scholars were required to room together. At Columbia, they were required to live on the campus, without the usual student right to commute from other living quarters.

This solicitude, the faculties soon recognized, was not unlike that of parents with their first infant, resulting in the same anxious overprotection. The situation was well illustrated at one college where an all-Scholar dormitory was nicknamed "The Nursery." It was soon recognized that these special arrangements, like those in the academic sphere, had been unwise, and they too were in almost all cases withdrawn. The colleges, like parents with their later children, have been a great deal more relaxed in their handling of subsequent Scholar groups.

While academic counseling has been available at all institutions, provision for trained guidance on personal and social problems has been less common. At a majority of the institutions Scholars have shared counseling services available to all students. A few colleges assigned special counselors to the Scholars. At least one of these, however, withdrew this service after the first year on the grounds that the program should "stand on its own feet."

THE ACADEMIC PREPARATION OF THE SCHOLARS AND COMPARISONS

During their first year of college, all four groups of Scholars and Comparison students were asked to list fields of study in which they felt handicapped by faulty or insufficient preparation in secondary school. A substantial proportion of all four groups of Scholars (ranging from 42 per cent to 54 per cent) reported no handicaps at all, despite the fact that most of them had not finished high school. On the other hand, a surprising proportion of the Comparison students (ranging from 40 per cent to 60 per cent) reported handicaps in one or more fields, despite the fact that they had entered college with four years of high school preparation. This is striking evidence of the unevenness of secondary school preparation in the United States and of the wide range in ability among high school students.

The 1951 and 1952 Scholars tended to report slightly more academic handicaps than their Comparison students, but in the case of the 1953 and 1954 groups, the proportion reporting handicaps was about the same for the Scholars as for the Comparison students. Mathematics and English Composition were the fields most frequently listed by Scholars and Comparison students alike in reporting handicaps due to faulty or insufficient preparation. (See Appendix Table IV, A.)

According to the judgment of the colleges, most of the Scholars and Comparison students had overcome their handicaps by the end of sophomore year. The proportion judged to have no gaps or omissions in their preparation still remaining at the end of sophomore year ranged from 88 per cent to 93 per cent among

[20]

the Scholars, and from 85 to 97 per cent among the Comparison students. (See Appendix Table IV, B.) These figures would indicate that in the judgment of the colleges, the Comparison students were slightly more successful than the Scholars in overcoming the deficiencies in their academic preparation, and that the overwhelming majority of both had succeeded in doing so.

A more subjective report on the matter of overcoming deficiencies in previous preparation was contained in the essays written by the 1951 and 1952 senior Scholars and Comparison students just before graduation. Both groups were asked, in looking back over their four-year college experience, if they had been handicapped by any deficiencies in their academic preparation for college. The answers tended to confirm what these same students had reported during their first year of college. Sixty-five per cent of the 1951 Scholars and 56 per cent of the 1952 Scholars reported handicaps in one or more fields, as against 52 per cent of the 1951 Comparison students and 60 per cent of the 1952 Comparison students. Then they were asked if they had been able to overcome their handicaps. Their replies tended to confirm what the colleges had reported. Ninety-two per cent of the 1951 Scholars and 93 per cent of the 1952 Scholars said they had overcome their handicaps in whole or in part, as against 90 per cent of the 1951 Comparison students and 95 per cent of the 1952 Comparison students.

Richard Pearson of the College Entrance Examination Board, who analyzed the essays of the 1951 and 1952 Scholars and Comparison students who graduated, suggested in his report that the initial deficiencies may well have turned out to be an added stimulus rather than a handicap to the Scholars. This underscored a point made by many of the senior Scholars in their essays, namely that they found in college an intellectual challenge and satisfaction that they had not been able to obtain in high school.

THE ACADEMIC PERFORMANCE

OF THE SCHOLARS

ONE OF THE BASIC questions raised by the Program for Early Admission to College was: How would the Scholars do academically, in view of their comparative youth and their less than normal high school preparation?

A preliminary answer to this question was given in *Bridging the Gap Between School and College*, published in the summer of 1953, which reported on the freshman year performance of the first group of Scholars. Briefly summarized, the preliminary results showed that the 1951 Scholars had outperformed not only their classmates, but also their Comparison students.

Now that four Scholar groups have entered the program and two have graduated, the evidence confirms and strengthens the preliminary findings.[1]

GRADE-POINT AVERAGES

It should probably come as no surprise that academically the Scholars as a group outperformed their classes as a whole by a wide margin. But offhand, one might expect the Comparison students to do better than the Scholars, in view of their advantage in age and high school preparation. This has not been the

[1] Some complications need to be reckoned with in interpreting the data in this chapter. Shimer, for example, did not establish Comparison groups and it deliberately selected Scholars with a wide range of academic aptitudes. At Fisk, the freshman and sophomore grades of the 1951 and 1952 groups of Scholars were not compared to the grades of the Comparison students because the Scholars took different kinds of courses. Finally, there was no formally designated "freshman class" at Chicago in 1951, so it was not possible to compare Scholar grades with Comparison student grades in that year.

CHART II

PER CENT OF SCHOLARS AND COMPARISONS
IN TOP HALF OF CLASS

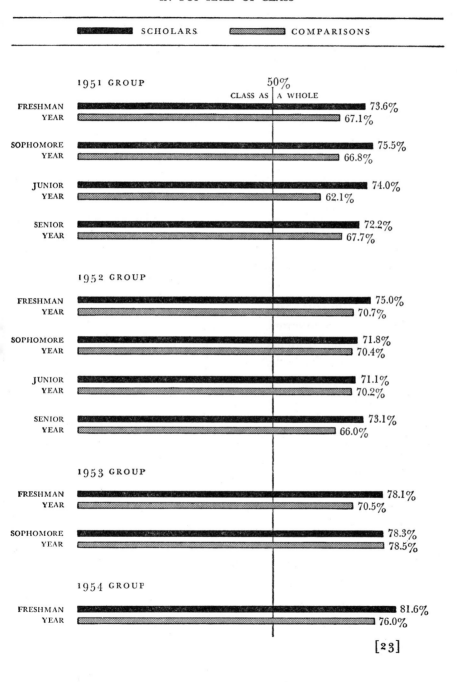

SCHOLARS   COMPARISONS

1951 GROUP   50%
                        CLASS AS | A WHOLE

FRESHMAN YEAR   73.6% / 67.1%

SOPHOMORE YEAR   75.5% / 66.8%

JUNIOR YEAR   74.0% / 62.1%

SENIOR YEAR   72.2% / 67.7%

1952 GROUP

FRESHMAN YEAR   75.0% / 70.7%

SOPHOMORE YEAR   71.8% / 70.4%

JUNIOR YEAR   71.1% / 70.2%

SENIOR YEAR   73.1% / 66.0%

1953 GROUP

FRESHMAN YEAR   78.1% / 70.5%

SOPHOMORE YEAR   78.3% / 78.5%

1954 GROUP

FRESHMAN YEAR   81.6% / 76.0%

[23]

case. Year after year, a higher proportion of Scholars than Comparison students ranked in the top tenth, fifth, and third of their classes. In all but six instances, a lower proportion of Scholars than Comparison students ranked in the bottom tenth of their classes. (See Appendix Table V, A.)

Chart II shows the proportion of Scholars and Comparison students with grade-point averages in the top half of their classes. (The comparative figure for the class as a whole in each case is 50 per cent.) As the chart indicates, the initial superiority of the 1951 Scholars over their class as a whole and over their Comparison students continued throughout their four years of college. The size of this "edge" fluctuated slightly from year to year, but it remained clear-cut and consistent. In freshman year, for example, nearly 74 per cent of the 1951 Scholars ranked in the top half of their class, as against 67 per cent of the Comparison students. In senior year, 72 per cent of the 1951 Scholars were in the top half of their class, as against 68 per cent of the Comparison students.

The Scholars who entered college in 1952 also outperformed their Comparison students and the class as a whole in each of their four years. Their "edge" over the Comparisons in freshman year was not as large as the one the 1951 Scholars had achieved over their Comparisons, and it dwindled further in the sophomore and junior years, but it expanded again in senior year to a point where it was larger than the senior year margin enjoyed by the 1951 Scholars.

The 1953 and 1954 Scholars did proportionately better in their freshman year than the 1951 and 1952 Scholars, and the margin of their superiority over their Comparison students was larger, but in sophomore year there was no significant difference between the performance of the 1953 Scholars and their Comparison students. (When this report was prepared, data were not yet available on the junior year grades of the 1953 Scholars and Comparisons, or the sophomore year grades of the 1954 Scholars and Comparisons.)

[24]

CHART III

HOW THE 1952 SCHOLARS AND COMPARISONS
RANKED IN THEIR CLASSES

SCHOLARS   COMPARISONS

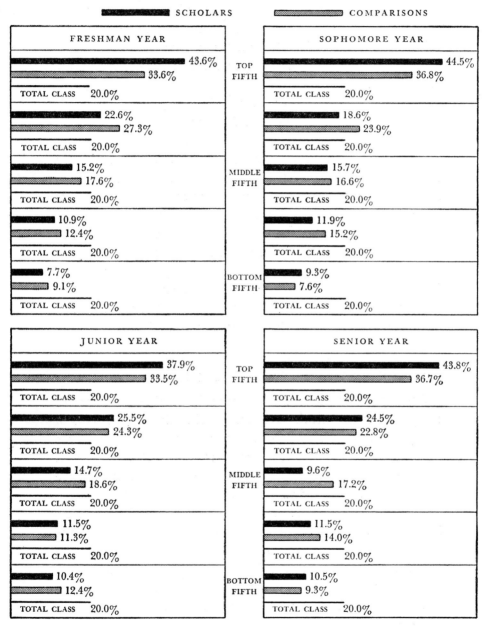

FRESHMAN YEAR

43.6%
33.6%
TOP FIFTH
TOTAL CLASS   20.0%

22.6%
27.3%
TOTAL CLASS   20.0%

15.2%
17.6%
MIDDLE FIFTH
TOTAL CLASS   20.0%

10.9%
12.4%
TOTAL CLASS   20.0%

7.7%
9.1%
BOTTOM FIFTH
TOTAL CLASS   20.0%

SOPHOMORE YEAR

44.5%
36.8%
TOTAL CLASS   20.0%

18.6%
23.9%
TOTAL CLASS   20.0%

15.7%
16.6%
TOTAL CLASS   20.0%

11.9%
15.2%
TOTAL CLASS   20.0%

9.3%
7.6%
TOTAL CLASS   20.0%

JUNIOR YEAR

37.9%
33.5%
TOP FIFTH
TOTAL CLASS   20.0%

25.5%
24.3%
TOTAL CLASS   20.0%

14.7%
18.6%
MIDDLE FIFTH
TOTAL CLASS   20.0%

11.5%
11.3%
TOTAL CLASS   20.0%

10.4%
12.4%
BOTTOM FIFTH
TOTAL CLASS   20.0%

SENIOR YEAR

43.8%
36.7%
TOP FIFTH
TOTAL CLASS   20.0%

24.5%
22.8%
TOTAL CLASS   20.0%

9.6%
17.2%
MIDDLE FIFTH
TOTAL CLASS   20.0%

11.5%
14.0%
TOTAL CLASS   20.0%

10.5%
9.3%
BOTTOM FIFTH
TOTAL CLASS   20.0%

Chart III (page 25) shows the actual distribution of grade-point averages for the 1952 Scholars and Comparisons. This group was chosen for illustrative purposes because it is the largest for which comparable data are available (414 Scholars and 431 Comparison students at 11 colleges in the freshman year, and 277 Scholars and 309 Comparison students at 11 colleges in the senior year).

As the chart indicates, a substantially larger proportion of Scholars than Comparisons ranked in the top fifth of their class in all four years of college, while the situation at the bottom end of the scale was mixed. In the freshman and junior years, a slightly lower proportion of Scholars than Comparisons ranked in the bottom fifth of the class, but in the sophomore and senior years the situation was reversed.

Scholars with 11 years of previous schooling tended to do slightly better than those with only ten, but the latter tended to do slightly better than those with 12. Among all four groups of Scholars, those with only ten years of previous schooling tended to rank in the top fifth of their class with greater frequency than the Comparison students. (See Appendix Table V, B.)

AREA TESTS OF THE
GRADUATE RECORD EXAMINATIONS

Grade-point averages are a reasonably reliable yardstick for comparing the academic performance of individual students or groups of students *within* a college or university, but they are not very reliable in measuring the comparative performance of students in *several* institutions, because each institution may be using a different yardstick.

In the spring of 1954, however, the Educational Testing Service of Princeton, New Jersey, made available a new battery of tests that provided a much broader basis for measuring the comparative performance of the Scholars and Comparison students at the 12 participating colleges and universities. These new tests were the Area Tests of the Graduate Record Examinations, which had been in the process of development for several years and which ETS described as "entirely new measures of unusual scope designed to assess the broad outcomes of education in the liberal arts." These tests, covering the Humanities, Natural Science, and Social Science, were aimed far beyond the details of specific courses and were intended to measure the student's grasp of basic concepts in the liberal arts and his ability to apply them.

From the standpoint of the Early Admission experiment, these new tests offered two distinct advantages: (1) they represented a much stiffer challenge than existing standardized tests (the Scholars and Comparisons had been bumping their heads on the ceilings of these tests), and (2) they made it possible not only to measure the performance of Scholars and Comparison students at all of the participating institutions with a uniform yardstick, but also to compare the performance of both groups with that of students in other American colleges, as the tests were available to colleges and universities throughout the country.

Through the co-operation of ETS, arrangements were made to have the GRE Area Tests administered to the Scholars and Comparison students in the 12 colleges and universities participating in the Early Admission experiment. First to take the new tests were the 1952 Scholars and Comparisons, who were then in their sophomore year. Each Scholar and Comparison group has taken these tests at least once, and the 1952 Scholars and Comparisons took them twice—first at the end of sophomore year, and again at the end of senior year. The 1951 Scholars and Comparisons took the tests as seniors, and the 1953 and 1954 Scholars and Comparisons took them as sophomores. It is planned to have these two latter groups take the tests again as seniors.

Chart IV (page 28) summarizes the results of the testings to date. As it indicates, each group of Scholars outperformed its Comparison group, both in terms of mean scaled scores and also in terms of the proportion scoring above 500, which was the estimated mean (average score) on each test for a "standardization" group of college seniors.

[27]

CHART IV

SOPHOMORE AND SENIOR SCORES ON GRE AREA TESTS

Bar shows relative mean scaled scores; figures at left give exact mean scaled scores.
▼
Figures in right column are percentage scoring above 500.
▼

SOPHOMORE SCORES:

Social Science	1952 SCHOLARS	558	74%
	1952 COMPAR.	527	64%
Humanities	1952 SCHOLARS	575	77%
	1952 COMPAR.	540	63%
Natural Science	1952 SCHOLARS	598	82%
	1952 COMPAR.	576	73%
Social Science	1953 SCHOLARS	512	57%
	1953 COMPAR.	504	54%
Humanities	1953 SCHOLARS	550	63%
	1953 COMPAR.	529	59%
Natural Science	1953 SCHOLARS	539	60%
	1953 COMPAR.	529	57%
Social Science	1954 SCHOLARS	523	59%
	1954 COMPAR.	488	47%
Humanities	1954 SCHOLARS	564	72%
	1954 COMPAR.	525	54%
Natural Science	1954 SCHOLARS	569	75%
	1954 COMPAR.	537	58%

SENIOR SCORES:

Social Science	1951 SCHOLARS	620	88%
	1951 COMPAR.	557	65%
Humanities	1951 SCHOLARS	632	89%
	1951 COMPAR.	578	72%
Natural Science	1951 SCHOLARS	606	87%
	1951 COMPAR.	558	72%
Social Science	1952 SCHOLARS	608	88%
	1952 COMPAR.	579	77%
Humanities	1952 SCHOLARS	630	87%
	1952 COMPAR.	600	78%
Natural Science	1952 SCHOLARS	632	85%
	1952 COMPAR.	591	73%

The Scholars' margin of superiority over the Comparisons was clear and consistent, just as it was in the case of their grade-point averages. In each of the three areas covered by the tests, all four groups of Scholars had higher mean scores than their Comparison students, and a larger proportion of the Scholars than of the Comparisons scored above 500. There were, of course, wide variations between scores at the individual colleges. (See Appendix Table V, C.) There also were variations among the four groups of Scholars as a whole. The 1952 Scholars, for example, outperformed their 1953 and 1954 counterparts in each of the three test areas as sophomores, but as seniors were outperformed by the 1951 Scholars in two of the three test areas.

As might be expected, the Scholars and Comparisons scored higher on the Area Tests than other American college students. For example, all three groups of Scholars and Comparisons who took the tests as sophomores outscored other sophomores who took the tests, and the two groups of Scholars and Comparisons who took the tests as seniors outscored other college seniors who took the tests. This, of course, was not surprising, because the Scholars and Comparisons were well above average in scholastic aptitude. What did come as a surprise, however, was that all three of the Scholar and Comparison groups who took the tests as *sophomores* surpassed the test norms set by college *seniors* who took the tests—and by a wide margin. For example, when the 1952 Scholars and Comparisons took the tests as sophomores in the spring of 1954, the tests also were given to 3,035 liberal arts seniors at 21 colleges and universities not participating in the Early Admission experiment. The comparative results are shown on the following page.

In 1955, the Area Tests also were administered to 672 first-year graduate students at eight universities not participating in the Early Admission Program, and in 1956 to 1,201 first-year graduate students at 11 such universities. When the scores of the Scholars and Comparison students who took the tests as *sophomores* were compared to the scores of these *first-year graduate*

SOPHOMORE SCORES OF 1952 SCHOLARS AND COMPARISONS AS COMPARED TO SCORES OF OTHER COLLEGE SENIORS

	SOCIAL SCIENCE		HUMANITIES		NATURAL SCIENCE	
	Mean Scaled Scores	Per Cent Scoring Above 500	Mean Scaled Scores	Per Cent Scoring Above 500	Mean Scaled Scores	Per Cent Scoring Above 500
1952 SCHOLARS (SOPHOMORES)	558	74	575	77	598	82
1952 COMPARISONS (SOPHOMORES)	527	64	540	63	576	73
SENIORS AT OTHER COLLEGES	489	40	494	39	487	38

students, it was found that Scholars and Comparisons once again came out on top, the Scholars by a wider margin than the Comparisons. The results were as follows:

SOPHOMORE SCORES OF SCHOLARS AND COMPARISONS AS COMPARED TO SCORES OF FIRST–YEAR GRADUATE STUDENTS

		SOCIAL SCIENCE		HUMANITIES		NATURAL SCIENCE	
		Mean Scaled Scores	Per Cent Scoring Above 500	Mean Scaled Scores	Per Cent Scoring Above 500	Mean Scaled Scores	Per Cent Scoring Above 500
1952 SCHOLARS		558	74	575	77	598	82
1952 COMPARISONS		527	64	540	63	576	73
1953 SCHOLARS	SOPHOMORES	512	57	550	63	539	60
1953 COMPARISONS		504	54	529	59	529	57
1954 SCHOLARS		523	59	564	72	569	75
1954 COMPARISONS		488	47	525	54	537	58
672 FIRST-YEAR GRADUATE STUDENTS, 1955		486	48	482	44	489	47
1,201 FIRST-YEAR GRADUATE STUDENTS, 1956		479	47	484	45	502	49

These results offer striking evidence of the wide diversity in performance among American college students. They also raise

[30]

some basic and provocative questions. For example, even after making due allowance for the fact that the Scholars were exceptionally able students, and for the fact that the Early Admission colleges as a group are probably of higher quality than the cross-section of American colleges represented by the seniors and first-year graduate students whose test scores were reported above, the fact remains that the Scholars—after a less than normal high school preparation and only two years of college—demonstrated that they had a better grasp of the basic concepts of a liberal education than a large body of American college seniors and first-year graduate students. What are the implications of this for the conventional "lock step" system, which requires as a general rule that a student spend 16 years in school and college in order to earn a bachelor's degree? Should such students receive their degree as soon as they demonstrate sufficient competence to earn it, and then be allowed to get on with their graduate or professional work? (This actually did happen in some instances, notably at Chicago and Wisconsin. Two of the 1951 Scholars at Wisconsin, for example, compressed high school and college into five years and graduated with Phi Beta Kappa honors.)

There are no simple answers to the questions posed by the Scholars' impressive performance on the GRE Area Tests, but the comparative results suggest that such questions need serious examination—at the college level, and at the secondary school level as well.

When the 1952 Scholars and Comparisons took the Area Tests again as seniors, their performance indicated that their last two years of college were far from wasted. ETS made a special analysis of the results, focussing only on the 215 Scholars and 133 Comparisons who actually had taken the tests twice (a different form of each test was used each time). This analysis showed that both the Scholars and Comparisons "grew" substantially between the sophomore and senior year, and that the growth among the Scholars was comparatively greater than that among the Comparisons. The following table shows the increase in test scores:

GAIN IN TEST SCORES OF
1952 SCHOLARS AND COMPARISONS

	SOPHOMORE TESTING	SENIOR TESTING	GAIN
SOCIAL SCIENCE:			
SCHOLARS	564	609	45
COMPARISONS	528	575	47
HUMANITIES:			
SCHOLARS	580	632	52
COMPARISONS	559	600	41
NATURAL SCIENCE:			
SCHOLARS	598	635	37
COMPARISONS	579	590	11

The amount of "growth" varied from student to student, from college to college, and from test area to test area, but the over-all gain was particularly significant in view of the high plateau from which it was achieved. (The sophomore mean scores of the Scholars and Comparisons, it will be recalled, were substantially higher than the scores of a representative body of college *seniors*.) The fact that the Scholars showed substantially more growth than the Comparison students in the natural science field may be due in large measure to the fact that a larger proportion of Scholars than Comparisons majored in this field.

Several plausible explanations for the Scholars' consistent academic superiority over their Comparison students have been suggested, and there may be others. The first is that the Scholars have perhaps been more strongly motivated than the Comparison students and in many cases have had the additional incentive of wishing to keep their Fund scholarships. (Although some institutions were able to match their Scholars to Comparison students who were also on scholarship, this was not possible in all cases.)

Another is that aptitude scores, according to such limited research as has been accomplished to date, have a tendency to increase somewhat with age among students at this level. In other words, a 16-year-old Scholar with the same aptitude score as an 18-year-old Comparison student may in fact have a higher "real aptitude," and when he reaches 18 will have a higher aptitude score. Most of the colleges did not attempt to compensate for this, as the rate of increase is not sufficiently uniform to permit a reliable adjustment factor. Where an adjustment was made, however, the Scholars, for some unexplained reason, still did better than the Comparison students. For example, Chicago made a special effort to match each 1951 Scholar to a Comparison student whose aptitude score was from three to five points higher. Despite this compensatory arrangement, the grade-point averages attained by the 1951 Scholars were notably higher than those of the 1951 Comparison students in every year, and the Scholars outperformed the Comparisons on the GRE Area Tests.

A third explanation is that the Scholars, having left high school and entered college early, did not lose the intellectual momentum that is often lost by able students held fast by the "lock step" in an unchallenging academic environment.

Finally, it has been suggested that the "halo effect" of the experiment itself—the Scholars' awareness that their academic performance was being compared to that of the Comparison students—spurred them on to greater efforts.

In any event, the superior academic performance of all four groups of Scholars demonstrates that the ability to do well in college is not solely a function of chronological age or twelve years of previous preparation.

ACADEMIC HONORS AND DISTINCTIONS

The 1951 and 1952 Scholars who graduated from college won a disproportionate share of academic honors, prizes, fellowships, and other major awards. At practically all of the colleges where such data were available, the proportion of Scholars graduating with honors was higher than that for the Comparison students, and much higher than that for their classmates as a whole. The same was true of election to Phi Beta Kappa.

At Wisconsin, where the Scholars made an especially impressive academic record, nearly two thirds of the graduating Scholars in each group received honors, as against about one-third of the Comparisons and a fifth of the class as a whole. Twenty-six per cent of the 1951 Scholars and 30 per cent of the 1952 Scholars who graduated were elected to Phi Beta Kappa, as against 10 per cent of the 1951 Comparisons and 18 per cent of the 1952 Comparisons.

At Utah, the picture was substantially the same. Here, too, nearly two thirds of the graduating Scholars in each group received honors, as against 50 per cent of the 1951 Comparisons and 41 per cent of the 1952 Comparisons. Nine per cent of the 1951 Scholars and 22 per cent of the 1952 Scholars who graduated were elected to Phi Beta Kappa, as against 1.3 per cent and 5 per cent of their classmates.

At Chicago, nearly one third of each group of graduating Scholars received honors, a proportion substantially greater than that of the Comparison students. Of 12 student aides selected by the dean in 1955 to assist with official functions of the University (appointments made on the combined basis of scholarship and citizenship) fully half were 1951 Scholars. Two of the 1952 Scholars won National Science Foundation Fellowships, two won Woodrow Wilson Fellowships, and one won a Rhodes Scholarship.

One of the 1951 Scholars at Oberlin also won a Rhodes Scholarship.

Of the 11 students who in 1955 received the highest honors Columbia College bestows, three were members of the 1951 Scholar group. Sixteen of the 1952 Scholars graduated with honors and ten were elected to Phi Beta Kappa. By contrast, eight of the Comparisons received honors and seven were elected to Phi Beta Kappa.

Among the 1951 Scholars at Goucher, 14 out of the 19 appeared on the Dean's list for at least one year, and 13 were so cited in two or more years. Four received special honors at graduation and five were elected to Phi Beta Kappa. The 1951 Comparison group had only three Dean's scholars and only one of these was cited in more than one year. Two of the Comparisons received special honors at graduation, and two were elected to Phi Beta Kappa. Of the class entering in 1952, 12 Scholars were named on the Dean's list, nine of them for more than one year. Nine of the Comparison students were so honored, seven in more than one year.

One member of the 1951 Scholar group at Yale was made Class Orator, was awarded the highest academic prize which the University can bestow on an undergraduate, and was also awarded a fellowship for study in England upon graduation. Yale reported that in the opinion of the student body, as well as of the faculty of the college, he was considered the outstanding student in his class. One other member of the 1951 group received two academic prizes in his junior year and a third in his senior year, and still another was elected president of the Yale chapter of Phi Beta Kappa.

At Lafayette, four of the 21 Scholars who graduated in 1955 were elected to Phi Beta Kappa. This was especially significant because only 12 seniors in a class of more than 250 were accorded this honor. One of the Scholars received a Woodrow Wilson Fellowship, another received the National Science Association Fellowship, and a third was awarded a Fulbright Scholarship. Two of the Scholars who graduated in 1956 were elected to Phi Beta Kappa, and one was awarded a National Science Foundation Fellowship for graduate study.

A high proportion of the 1951 and 1952 Scholars who graduated indicated that they planned to go on to graduate work. The proportion varied from college to college, but overall it was 65 per cent for the 1951 Scholars who graduated, and 76 per cent for the 1952 Scholars who graduated. The corresponding figures for the Comparison students were 49 per cent and 58 per cent. (See Appendix Table VII.) At Wisconsin and Chicago, several members of both Scholar groups finished their undergraduate work in less than four years and were already engaged in graduate study when their classmates received the bachelor's degree.

THE SOCIAL AND EMOTIONAL
ADJUSTMENT OF THE SCHOLARS

ALL COLLEGE-BOUND students face a problem of adjustment to life on the campus. Entering college usually involves the first prolonged separation from parents, and the first taste of responsibility for meeting life's problems without benefit of parental authority or guidance. Every freshman must learn to budget his time as between studies and social activities. Further, having parted company with boyhood associations of long standing, he is confronted with the need to establish another set of personal relationships. He must "find" himself in an entirely new community. For the majority of students, these problems of adjustment to college are readily solved, but they are nonetheless very real problems for virtually every student.

An appraisal of the social and emotional adjustment of the Early Admission students must start from this point of departure. The central question is not whether or not these younger students encountered adjustment problems, for all students do. Rather, it is whether the problems they encountered were significantly different or more severe than those they might have encountered had they entered college at the conventional age, and, if so, whether they were successful in meeting them.

The task of appraising social and emotional adjustment is a great deal more difficult than that of judging academic performance. No single type of evidence by itself provides an adequate basis for conclusions, nor are there available any satisfactory devices for achieving a neat statistical measurement. In the large majority of cases judgment must rest upon a careful weighing of several types of evidence. With this in mind, the Fund and the participating colleges arranged to have several types of evidence gathered and analyzed for this report.

One type concerns the extent to which the Scholar participates voluntarily in "extra-class" activities, such as organized sports, dramatics, student publications, social clubs and other activities involving group participation and opportunities for leadership. Another consists of the seasoned opinion of experienced members of the college staff who have had an opportunity to observe the Scholars in various situations over a period of time. These faculty members were asked to appraise the overall adjustment of the Scholars at the end of freshman year and again at the end of senior year.

Still another type of evidence was obtained from essays written by the 1951 and 1952 Scholars and Comparison students just before graduation and analyzed by Richard Pearson. Finally, there are the findings and conclusions of the team of trained psychiatrists, headed by Dr. Dana Farnsworth, who made an independent appraisal of the 1951 Scholars' social and emotional adjustment and a special analysis of the cases of Scholars who for one reason or another dropped out of their original college before graduation.

PARTICIPATION IN EXTRA-CURRICULAR ACTIVITIES

Adjustment to college is not a quantitative thing to be measured in terms of the number of offices a student holds or the number of student organizations he belongs to, but reports from the colleges indicate that the Scholars did not achieve their outstanding academic record at the expense of having to forego extra-class activities.

The Fund, at the end of the 1951 Scholars' freshman year, reported that they had participated in extra-class activities at least as extensively as their classmates. Recent reports from the colleges and universities covering the complete four-year experience of these Scholars and their 1952 counterparts indicate a still higher degree of sharing in the extra-curricular life of the campus.

Goucher reported that the Scholars took a more active part in extra-curricular activities and held more campus offices than their classmates. "The College considers them a most desirable leaven in the student body," the dean observed in her report. The University of Wisconsin also reported that its Scholars were on the average more active than their classmates, citing their participation in the band, orchestra, theater group, campus paper (of which two Scholars were associate editors), humor magazine, and yearbook.

Yale was the only institution to report that its Scholars may have been less active than their classmates, but it noted that the difference was slight. Fisk reported that the 1951 Scholar group was less active in extra-curricular organizations than succeeding groups, but that the leadership of these latter groups "has stimulated these organizations very distinctly."

Utah, Oberlin, and Shimer reported that the Scholars' extra-curricular activity was about equal to that of their classmates. At Oberlin, one 1951 Scholar was elected president of the Student Association in his senior year. At Columbia, one 1951 Scholar was editor of the humor magazine *Jester,* another was managing editor of the *Spectator,* and a third was co-manager of the football team. Lafayette also reported a high degree of extra-curricular activity. Scholars there were members of eight varsity athletic squads. One was a Deacon and Elder of the College Church, another was business manager of the choir, and many participated in radio, debating, and dramatics. Chicago reported that the leadership of the Scholars was felt in every major area of extra-curricular activities.

FACULTY RATINGS OF OVER-ALL ADJUSTMENT

Each of the participating colleges and universities was asked to have faculty members who were most familiar with the Scholars and Comparison students appraise their over-all adjust-

[38]

ment to college life, first at the end of freshman year and again at the end of senior year. Each college was asked to obtain independent ratings on each student from two or more faculty members or college officials familiar with the student. It was suggested that where differences of opinion occurred they should be resolved by an appropriate person at the college who would make a composite rating. The check-list of factors to be taken into consideration in rating the students included such items as poise and self-confidence in social situations, leadership ability, study habits, participation in group activity, gregariousness, personal appearance, degree of dependence on family, worry and emotional control, adjustment to the opposite sex, ease in conversation, academic program planning, and educational interests.

At the End of Freshman Year

The faculty ratings of the four Scholar and Comparison groups at the end of freshman year were as follows:

RATING OF ADJUSTMENT AT END OF FRESHMAN YEAR

RATING	1951 GROUP		1952 GROUP		1953 GROUP		1954 GROUP	
	Scholars	*Compar.*	*Scholars*	*Compar.*	*Scholars*	*Compar.*	*Scholars*	*Compar.*
EXCELLENT	23.4%	21.7%	15.3%	16.6%	15.7%	12.5%	17.9%	11.1%
GOOD	38.9	45.4	45.8	47.5	52.8	60.0	55.8	58.3
MODERATELY GOOD	26.0	25.4	29.8	28.7	23.6	25.0	18.8	27.1
POOR	10.2	7.1	7.6	7.0	5.7	2.5	6.7	2.8
VERY POOR	1.5	.4	1.5	.3	2.2		.9	.7

As the table indicates, the over-all adjustment of the overwhelming majority of Scholars and Comparisons in each group was rated either "moderately good," "good," or "excellent," and with a slight exception in the case of the 1951 Scholars, less than 10 per cent of each group received ratings of "poor" or "very poor." There was a wider "scatter" in the Scholar ratings, and the Comparison students as a whole were found by the faculties to have adjusted better—although not a great deal better—than the Scholars.

At the End of Senior Year

At the end of their senior year, the 1951 and 1952 Scholars and Comparison students were rated once again by their faculties. The results were as follows:

RATING OF ADJUSTMENT AT END OF SENIOR YEAR

| | 1951 GROUP | | 1952 GROUP | |
RATINGS	SCHOLARS	COMPARISONS	SCHOLARS	COMPARISONS
EXCELLENT	23.6%	26.4%	20.6%	20.5%
GOOD	46.5	43.7	46.8	59.3
MODERATELY GOOD	22.8	23.4	25.8	16.7
POOR	5.1	4.6	6.0	2.7
VERY POOR	2.0	2.0	.7	.8

As the table indicates, the proportion of Scholars and Comparisons rated at the top of the scale in this final appraisal was higher than had been the case at the end of freshman year. Most of the difference is undoubtedly accounted for by the fact that many of the Scholars and Comparison students who had made a poor initial adjustment had withdrawn from college before the end of senior year. Once again the results showed that in the judgment of the faculties, the Comparison students as a group had made a slightly better adjustment than the Scholars, but that well over 90 per cent of both groups had adjusted moderately well or better.

It should be noted that there were variations among Scholars on different campuses, and among individual Scholars on the same campus. Scholars on some campuses, often for special reasons, had more difficult adjustment problems than other students. Yale, for example, reported that its 1951 Scholars had more difficulties than their classmates in adjustment to college in general and to Yale in particular. Yale noted that this was partly due to the fact that, as a matter of policy, it selected a number of Scholars from rural backgrounds. Columbia made a similar comment about extra difficulties encountered by rural students on its large urban campus.

Louisville reported that social and emotional adjustment on its campus was made more difficult by the fact that out-of-town Scholars were housed in dormitories, where there was little social activity because most Louisville students live at home. Adjustment at Wisconsin appears to have been made more difficult by the fact that most of the 1951 and 1952 Scholars were not residents of the state and had to be lodged in rooming houses in compliance with a state law which restricts occupancy of dormitories to residents of the state. Fisk reported that the adjustment of its 1951 Scholars was not so good as that of later groups because they were chosen with relative haste and were separated from other students during the first year.

While some colleges and universities commented that the Scholars' youth and early admission may have accentuated their initial adjustment difficulties, they reported that in most cases the difficulties were subsequently overcome. In the few cases of social or emotional maladjustment that did develop, early admission was not considered the determining factor. Chicago expressed itself most strongly on this point. Commenting on the similarity of the Scholars' difficulties to those of regular students, the dean of the college said in his report to the Fund: "I have not seen a single Scholar who had serious psychological problems of whom I felt that they would *not* have occurred if he had remained at home another year or two."

THE STUDENTS' OWN TESTIMONY

The 1951 and 1952 Scholars and Comparisons who successfully completed their undergraduate work were asked in their senior year to take a retrospective look at their four-year college experience and to answer candidly and thoughtfully a series of essay questions. They were assured that their replies would be kept confidential, and were urged to be free and frank in their comments.

One of the questions they were asked was: "Apart from any deficiencies in your preparation, did you encounter any difficulties in adjusting to the academic or social aspects of college life?"

The responses were as follows:

| | 1951 GROUP | | 1952 GROUP | |
	SCHOLARS	COMPARISONS	SCHOLARS	COMPARISONS
YES	81%	52%	63%	51%
NO	19	47	37	49
NO RESPONSE	—	1	—	—

These responses tend to support the belief of the colleges that the restrictive measures applied to the "pioneer" group of 1951 Scholars added to their adjustment problems, and that removal of these restrictions made things easier for succeeding Scholar groups.

The difficulty most frequently cited by the Scholars was that they had felt "bashful," "shy," "immature," or had "taken time to make friends." Nearly a third of them volunteered that this had been the case. Roughly a quarter of them mentioned specific trouble with "dating." Another 25 per cent cited a difficulty that was unique to the Scholars: they felt that they were considered by regular students as members of an "out group."

The Comparison students reported that they too had suffered from "shyness," "immaturity," "slowness to make friends," and difficulty with dating. However, the proportion citing these difficulties was markedly lower than for the Scholars. In general, the Comparison students reported somewhat less trouble of a strictly social and emotional nature and somewhat more trouble with study habits and with budgeting their time as between social and academic activities.

A more detailed examination of the Scholars' social and emotional problems may logically begin with the only important difficulty which was unique to the 1951 and 1952 Scholars—a feeling of exclusion from normal college activities which arose from the fact that they were members of a special, experimental group. This feeling, felt most acutely by the 1951 Scholars in their freshman year, was described by one of them in these words: "The rest of the freshman class seemed to adopt the attitude that we were a novel type of insect which should be studied with great concentration during the time that you were not actually poking it with a stick." Although this is probably an exaggeration, it illustrates the initial difficulty many of the 1951 Scholars encountered on some campuses before they finally won acceptance. As Pearson observed in his report: "The picture one obtains of this adjustment problem is that the Scholars entering college in 1951 had to live down an exaggerated and somewhat distorted idea of what the 'Fordie' was really like. Older classmates, faculty, and college administration expected the Scholars to be much more different from the regular than they really were. Their intellectual prowess was held in high and sometimes envious regard; their social inadequacies and physical immaturity were looked upon with considerable disdain."

The problem was greatly eased as soon as the institutions withdrew their segregating arrangements, and later classes of Scholars had far less of an obstacle to surmount in this respect. To quote the Pearson report: "By their intellectual and social accomplishments during the early years of college, the Scholars were generally able to convince their classmates that age was but one of the ways in which individuals differ." Pearson reported that the feeling of being members of an "out group" also was cited by a number of the 1952 Scholars. "The continuance of this as a significant complaint represents a shift among the participating colleges," he noted. "Yale, where this was a problem the first year and where sixteen such reports occurred a year ago, now produced only one such report. This improvement, however, was offset by the appearance of seven reports at Morehouse (which was not active during the first year of the experiment), and eight reports at Fisk (where not many essays were received from Scholars among the 1951 group)." Pearson concluded that "these problems have not materially lessened in the experiment as a whole, although progress is certainly noticeable at colleges where the experiment has been in operation since 1951."

Other difficulties encountered by the Scholars early in college differed from those of regular students in degree but not in kind. Pearson noted that the Scholars' youthfulness may have accentuated their shyness—a problem of which regular students also complained, and it is certain that youthfulness accentuated the male Scholars' dating problem—a problem from which female Scholars were entirely free. One male Scholar told in his essay of a particularly harrowing experience with the "dating" problem:

I will never forget the occasion of the first freshman "mixer" expedition to a girl's college in which I participated—it was also the last for quite some time. I was getting along fairly well in my conversation with a young lady (of dubious charm, but a girl nevertheless, and on that occasion it was the only consideration which prevailed) for whose attentions I was competing with a "regular" freshman, when it came out that I was a Ford student of the tender age of 15—and by the way, I had *just* had my first introduction to the ritual of shaving. I received, in effect, a chilly "my, how . . . interesting," and the cause was lost. I was crushed for months.

Another gave the following account of the difficulties he encountered and how he coped with them:

I felt a social disadvantage with my classmates in the first year or two. Perhaps the stigma of "Ford Scholars" had something to do with this. Many mistakes were made in the early administration of the program (living together, etc.). Somewhat of an inability to completely integrate into the older group was experienced. In part, I would attribute this difficulty to the administration of the program in the freshman year. In some respects it is a deficiency of the program itself.

In social contacts with the opposite sex, I was obviously unable to date college freshmen when I entered at sixteen. Yet I did make contacts with local high school girls which helped to offset this problem. By sophomore year the problem all but vanished. Whatever difficulty there was might also be attributed to the program of early entrance.

None of the above-mentioned problems were of large proportions.

[44]

Little frustration developed, and, in retrospect, I indicate only some impressions rather than enormous difficulties.

Time and rapid development and maturing were the main factors in overcoming the difficulties. Within a year I was sufficiently adjusted and confident of myself to make new acquaintances and relationships among my classmates. Once on my own and away from the "group of Ford Scholars" I was as integrated as any of my classmates. The placement of Ford students together was the major factor in the difficulty. Once this ceased, the problem quickly disappeared.

Reports from the colleges also mentioned the male Scholars' dating problem. One college observed: "The boys work hard at strange shifts to conceal their age, since no girl who values her reputation wants a date with a boy two years her junior." While many Comparison students also complained that they had been "cold-shouldered" by freshman girls during their first year, the Scholars' difficulty in this respect was more acute.

Perhaps the most eloquent testimony that dating was not much of a problem for the girls in the Early Admission Program came from the 1951 Scholar who wrote in the summer of 1955:

I have participated in social activities fully, having no inclination to be "bookish" as some of my Ford colleagues definitely are. Perhaps my social adjustment can be best characterized by the fact that I dated frequently (and variously!) during my first two years, settling down to a fiancé in my junior year, marrying him in the early part of last June, and becoming a mother this past March 28!

In their essay questionnaires at the end of senior year, the Scholars and Comparisons also were asked whether they had been able to overcome their social and emotional difficulties. The responses, based on the total number who had reported difficulties, were as follows:

| | 1951 GROUP | | 1952 GROUP | |
	SCHOLARS	COMPARISONS	SCHOLARS	COMPARISONS
YES	73%	57%	80%	87%
PARTLY	17	22	14	9
NO	7	15	5	2
NO RESPONSE	3	6	1	2

These responses would indicate that in the judgment of the students themselves, the 1951 Scholars were more successful in overcoming their adjustment difficulties than their Comparison students, and that the 1952 Scholars were somewhat less successful than their Comparison students, but considerably more successful than the 1951 Scholars.

THE FINDINGS OF THE PSYCHIATRISTS

The team of psychiatrists headed by Dr. Farnsworth, in seeking to judge the social and emotional adjustment of the 1951 Scholars, began by examining their performance from the negative point of view. They made a careful study of the incidence of neurotic or psychotic symptoms among the Scholars with a view to comparing this with the incidence found among regular college students. This determination was, of course, highly important, for a possible hazard of early admission could be that it would submit the young Scholars to excessive psychological strain.

The finding of the psychiatrists, based on all available student records as well as on personal interviews with some of the Scholars, was most definite on this score. The Scholar group, they reported, showed no more psychiatric difficulties than the older Comparison students. The few psychotic cases which developed among the Scholars were, according to the psychiatrists, no more than is normally found in this age group. As for the proportion of cases of "simple adolescent maladjustment," this also was small and at no college exceeded that of the Comparison students. Nor did the 1951 Scholars, in general, exhibit more difficulty than the Comparison students because of "emotional immaturity."

The Farnsworth team found that the proportion of Scholars visiting college and university counseling services for help with emotional difficulties was the same as or lower than that for college students in general. The number of Scholar visits to college medical services was also examined for possible indication of psychosomatic ailments because, as the report observed: "It is

[46]

well known that frequent visits by a student to the college health service for minor physical complaints are apt to mean that the student is actually having emotional problems." The rate of Scholar visits was found to be no higher than that of their class-mates at any of the 11 institutions.

Proceeding to an evaluation of the Scholars' adjustment in the positive sense, Dr. Farnsworth and his colleagues emphasized the complexity of weighing over-all results in view of the diverse social and academic climates found on the eleven campuses. They noted that values and hence standards of adjustment were hardly uniform among the participating institutions. At some colleges and universities, the psychiatrists found "both the faculty and students place too great an emphasis on interpersonal relations, on being a 'good fellow' and on being 'well-rounded' at the ex-pense of educational values." As an extreme example of this, they cited the attitude of students at one institution who expressed doubt in interviews as to whether the Scholars could adequately participate in social activities "as among other things they were too young on moral grounds to take a drink."

On such a campus, the psychiatrists observed, "failure to con-form to social mores is apt to be severely penalized by the other students." Such a climate, however, did not prevail at most of the institutions participating in the Early Admission Program. Generally speaking, social activities at these colleges were not considered as ends in themselves, but as one of several means of facilitating mature development.

At the outset, the members of the Farnsworth team defined satisfactory adjustment to college in these terms:

What is desirable is not adjustment to the group at all costs, not good interpersonal relations in all situations, but real autonomy, i.e. men sufficiently free from both social and cultural pressures and from their own inner biases, needs and drives that they are able to assess the realities of situations and act on this basis. Although such men prize warm interpersonal relations and getting along with the group as a satisfactory part of living, they are not ends in themselves.

[47]

In reviewing the Scholars' problems, the Farnsworth team noted that the special academic and social arrangements made for the Scholars at some institutions the first year of the experiment frequently aroused "resentment, bitterness and hostility" in the Scholars. These feelings, they continued, resulted from the desire on the part of the students to be accepted by their peers, and their desire not to be stereotyped as the "scholarly type" or as "babies."

"The excessive concern of the faculties for the Scholars," the psychiatrists said, "was similar to that in 1945 when the veterans returned to the campuses. In both cases, the expectations were not realized; the students did well. . . . As a result of the excellent adjustment of the Scholars during the first year, the subsequent groups of Scholars were handled in a much more relaxed manner by the faculties."

The Farnsworth team found only two areas in which the Scholars experienced some difficulties in excess of their Comparison students and classmates. One was in the matter of dating during their freshman and sophomore years, and the other in securing employment during summer vacations. The men experienced the dating difficulties and the girls the vocational difficulties.

On the vocational difficulty, Farnsworth and his colleagues noted that most college students work during their summer vacations. The male Scholars had no difficulty finding jobs on a par with their older classmates, but such was not the case with the girls, many of whom could not get jobs because of their age. This, they found, was a source of unhappiness to some, but it was only a limited problem and did not unduly affect their college adjustment.

As for the dating problem, the psychiatrists found that it was a source of unhappiness to some male Scholars early in college. "Many boys spoke of the difficulties of obtaining dates with college girls during their freshman and sophomore years," they noted. "Difficulty in getting women college freshmen to date them was not confined to the freshman Scholars. In general, such

[48]

girls are more interested in upper classmen or graduate students. In the case of the Early Admission men, this difficulty in finding dates because of age extended beyond their first year, whereas in their older classmates the problem was usually solved by the time they were sophomores."

By junior year, Dr. Farnsworth and his colleagues found, the dating difficulty was surmounted and male Scholars had no further difficulties in getting dates. "Most Scholars during their junior and senior years, in the matter of dating, functioned on the level of their older classmates," they reported, "rather than that of the average freshmen who were their chronological age." Summing up, the Farnsworth team said it found "no evidence that these difficulties in dating in any way retarded their emotional development."[1]

The psychiatrists found no other area in which the difficulties of the Scholar group were different from those of regular students either in kind or degree. They did note that the Scholars of unusually youthful appearance had a harder time making the needed social adjustment than those who appeared on casual observation to be of the usual college entrance age, and suggested that students who "look like youngsters" should be warned before being allowed to enter college early that they may encounter more difficulty than others.

FAILURES, WITHDRAWALS, AND TRANSFERS

Of the 860 Scholars who entered the twelve participating colleges in 1951 and 1952, about 6 per cent failed academically and another 6 per cent failed because of adjustment difficulties.

The failure rate varied considerably from college to college. (See Appendix Table VI, C.) Over-all it was higher among the Scholars in each group than among their Comparison students, but the over-all picture did not hold true at all of the colleges.

[1] An interesting sidelight on the dating problem was reported by Wisconsin. Six or eight of its male Scholars have already married, and another dozen or so are engaged. Almost all have chosen girls older than themselves, since these were the girls they dated in college.

At three of the ten colleges where comparable data were available for 1951 Scholars and Comparison students (Morehouse did not enter the program until 1952, and Shimer did not establish Comparison groups) there were proportionately fewer failures among the Scholars than among the Comparisons, and at two others the proportion was about the same. The picture among the 1952 Scholars and Comparisons was substantially similar.

Six of the colleges compared the failure rate among the Scholars and Comparison students with that among their classmates as a whole. As the following table indicates, the proportion of Scholar failures was lower than that of their classmates at four of the six colleges.

PER CENT OF FAILURES AMONG SCHOLARS,
COMPARISONS AND CLASSMATES AT 6 COLLEGES

COLLEGE	1951 GROUP		
	SCHOLARS	COMPARISONS	CLASSMATES
GOUCHER	5.3%	10.6%	7.0%
LAFAYETTE	13.4	10.0	26.0
LOUISVILLE	6.9	0.0	6.0
OBERLIN	8.0	6.7	15.0
SHIMER	8.8	No Comparisons	10.6
YALE	19.2	7.8	9.2
	1952 GROUP		
GOUCHER	0.0	0.0	3.7
LAFAYETTE	17.3	10.3	29.0
LOUISVILLE	34.5	15.4	6.0
OBERLIN	13.7	5.4	15.0
SHIMER	6.2	No Comparisons	21.6
YALE	12.7	6.8	9.7

Proportionately fewer Scholars than Comparison students withdrew from college for reasons other than failure—to enter military service, to get married, because of illness or financial difficulty, or because of miscellaneous or unknown reasons.

Among the 1951 group the proportion was 11.4 per cent for the Scholars and 14.9 per cent for the Comparisons, and among the 1952 group it was 8.6 per cent for the Scholars and 13.6 per cent among the Comparisons. The data on this point do not offer any definite clues as to why the proportion was substantially less among the 1952 Scholars than among their 1951 counterparts.

The proportion of Scholars who transferred to other institutions was considerably higher than that of the Comparisons—15.2 per cent among the 1951 Scholars and 11.8 per cent among the 1952 Scholars, as against 5.8 per cent and 6.1 per cent among the two groups of Comparison students. Once again the picture varied considerably from college to college (see Appendix Table VI, C), and once again there were several colleges where the over-all generalization did not hold true. Special factors at several of the colleges tended to raise the over-all transfer rate for Scholars. At Shimer, for example, about one fifth of the 1951 and 1952 Scholars transferred to the University of Chicago after sophomore year to take specialized courses, which is customary among Shimer students. At Fisk, more than 35 per cent of the 1951 Scholars transferred to other institutions largely because of dissatisfaction with the rigorous first-year arrangements under which Scholars were separated from their classmates socially and academically. These restrictions were relaxed after the first year, and the transfer rate among the 1952 Scholars at Fisk dropped to only 3 per cent, which was less than the rate for the Comparison students. Wisconsin had an unusually high transfer rate among its 1951 and 1952 Scholars because more than half of them came from New York and New Jersey, and many of these Easterners later transferred to colleges closer to home. Beginning in 1953, Wisconsin no longer made a special effort to attract Early Admission candidates from schools outside the state.

A summary picture of the total attrition rate among the 1951 and 1952 Scholars and Comparison students is presented in the following table.

ATTRITION RATE AMONG
1951 AND 1952 SCHOLARS AND COMPARISON STUDENTS

| | 1951 GROUP | | | | 1952 GROUP | | | |
| | SCHOLARS | | COMPARISONS | | SCHOLARS | | COMPARISONS | |
	NO.	%	NO.	%	NO.	%	NO.	%
(NUMBER IN ENTERING CLASS)	(420)		(415)		(440)		(472)	
FAILED	47	11.2	34	8.2	55	12.5	46	9.8
WITHDREW FOR REASONS OTHER THAN FAILURE	48	11.4	62	14.9	38	8.6	64	13.6
TRANSFERRED	64	15.2	24	5.8	52	11.8	29	6.1
TOTAL ATTRITION	159	37.8	120	28.9	145	32.9	139	29.5

Dr. Farnsworth and his colleagues were asked by the Fund to make a detailed study of the failures, withdrawals, and transfers among the 1951 Scholars with special emphasis on a search for the underlying reasons. Members of the Farnsworth team visited the participating colleges, examined the records on each student, and interviewed faculty members who had taught the Scholars, student advisers, administration officials, classmates, and in some instances the Scholars themselves.

Unfortunately, it was not possible to make a similar study of the underlying reasons for failures, withdrawals, and transfers among the 1951 Comparison students. Because of the great interest of the faculty in the Early Admission students, much more information was available on them than on the Comparison students. Not only did the deans' offices accumulate voluminous records on the Scholars, but many members of the faculty were able to supply pertinent observations of their own. No such complete records were available on the Comparison students in most instances, and because the faculty had not known previously who the Comparison students were, they were unable to comment on them except in a cursory manner.

Members of the Farnsworth team compiled detailed information on 147 of the 159 Scholars who entered the eleven colleges in 1951 and subsequently failed, withdrew, or transferred to other institutions. In each case they went beyond the apparent reason to try to determine the basic underlying reason. The accompanying table shows the results of their findings.

PSYCHIATRISTS' CLASSIFICATION OF
REASONS FOR FAILURES, WITHDRAWALS, AND TRANSFERS
AMONG 1951 SCHOLARS

| | FAILURES AND WITHDRAWALS | | | | | | TRANSFERS | | |
COLLEGE	INADEQUATE INTELLECTUAL POTENTIAL	IMMATURITY WITH INADEQUATE GOAL-DIRECTED BEHAVIOR	PSYCHIATRIC DISORDER	INAPPROPRIATE VALUES	REALISTIC REASONS	MISCELLANEOUS	REALISTIC	VOCATIONAL	TOTAL
CHICAGO	0	6	4	0	1	0	0	1	12
COLUMBIA	0	2	3	2	1	1	0	0	9
FISK	1	5	2	1	0	2	5	2	18
GOUCHER	0	1	1	0	1	0	4	0	7
LAFAYETTE	0	0	1	3	0	1	1	2	8
LOUISVILLE	3	3	1	0	1	0	4	2	14
OBERLIN	0	2	1	0	0	0	3	2	8
SHIMER	4	4	2	1	2	0	5	3	21
UTAH	0	0	1	4	6	8	1	3	23
WISCONSIN	0	6	1	0	1	0	6	5	19
YALE	0	5	2	0	0	0	1	0	8
TOTAL	8	34	19	11	13	12	30	20	147

As the table indicates, the greatest loss of Scholars was through transfer to other institutions. Dr. Farnsworth and his colleagues found that two-fifths of these transfers were made for strictly vocational reasons. In some of these cases early admission was a contributing cause in the sense that the students had entered the program for the sole purpose of speeding their entry into professions or jobs. Having entered colleges requiring liberal arts courses, they often chafed at these courses and switched to more specialized professional or vocational schools. There were also other vocational transfers caused by an interest in some particular field which could not be met by any but a very specialized institution.

Three-fifths of the Scholar transfers were found to have been for "realistic" reasons, the same in nature as American student transfers generally, and in no way related to early admission. Some Scholars, for example, switched to colleges nearer home. An unusual number of these occurred at Wisconsin, for reasons mentioned earlier in this chapter. Other Scholars transferred because they had married and wanted to attend school where their husbands or wives were already studying. Still others with financial difficulties left to enter schools enabling them to save money by living at home. Commenting on the Scholar transfers as a whole, the Farnsworth team noted that "they do not represent an actual loss . . . as in almost all instances they will subsequently obtain degrees in other institutions."

The psychiatrists found that immaturity, characterized by what they termed "inadequate goal-directed behavior," was the major factor in the cases involving failure or withdrawal from college for reasons other than failure. Such cases were found at all but two of the participating institutions. Many of these Scholars had been classified by the deans' offices as academic failures, but the psychiatrists found that the root of their trouble was deeper.

In general such Scholars, despite their high academic promise, were found to have been unable to accept even a reasonable degree of self-management in the college setting. The Farnsworth team observed that many of them came from difficult family situations: "In some cases a parent was missing due to death or divorce; in others the parents were extremely protective or perfectionistic. In some cases, the fathers and mothers were extremely authoritarian and had allowed the student almost no freedom of individual expression prior to coming to college. In still other cases, the students did not want to come to college and were merely fulfilling their parents' expectations."

Dr. Farnsworth and his colleagues concluded that early admission to college was not the underlying reason for failure among such students. "Coming to college a year earlier merely precipitated their difficulties into the open," they observed. "It is difficult to believe that these students would have succeeded in college had they not entered the Early Admission Program, as this would have necessitated their remaining another year in their difficult home situation."

Did the Early Admission Program produce an unusually high proportion of "immature" students? The psychiatrists consider that it did not. Noting that most of the Scholars were 16 years old or younger and had not previously been away from home for an extended time, the Farnsworth team declared: "It is surprising that this figure was less than 10 per cent. Certainly it is the experience of colleges in admitting students two years older, that this large a percentage of them (8 per cent) are immature."

The second most important category of Scholar withdrawals, responsible for the loss of 6 per cent of the 1951 group, was found to consist of a variety of "realistic" and/or "miscellaneous" causes unrelated to early admission. For example, eight of the Utah Scholars left at the end of junior year to serve as missionaries of the Church of Jesus Christ of the Latter Day Saints. This is a customary expectation for young men of their faith, and past experience at Utah has been that such students return to college when their missionary work is completed. Other reasons for withdrawal in this category were death of an important family member, entrance into the military service, marriage, or family financial problems.

Dr. Farnsworth and his colleagues found that 5 per cent of the 1951 Scholars dropped out of college because of psychiatric disorders not related to early admission. Three of these cases were diagnosed as schizophrenia in which the difficulties far antedated the Scholars entrance into college. In five other cases, defined as "characteriological," the Scholars had exhibited aberrant behavior in secondary schools and their disorders had developed before they entered the campuses. Such Scholars, the Farnsworth team noted, represented errors in selection; had their records been known, they would not have been admitted.

As for the psychiatric withdrawals diagnosed as "simple adolescent maladjustment" cases, almost all came from difficult family situations, most often a broken home. Such cases, the psychiatrists reported, respond well to psychotherapy, and many students with such histories, who have been helped by treatment or who have recovered spontaneously have made outstanding contributions to the academic world. More adequate psychiatric counseling facilities on some campuses might have prevented some of these withdrawals, the report said.

Dr. Farnsworth and his colleagues found that the incidence of psychiatric difficulties—major or minor—was not greater among the Scholars than among regular students. They also reported that excluding the five Scholars diagnosed as having character neuroses, at least half of the remaining Scholars who left college because of psychiatric disorders later returned, usually to colleges less demanding than those at which their emotional difficulties had occurred.

About 3 per cent of the 1951 Scholars were found to have dropped out of college because of a lack of values appropriate for education. This phenomenon took a higher toll of the group than did lack of intellectual ability *per se*. Such Scholars showed almost no interest in acquiring a college education, did not study hard, were never concerned about their academic performance and were surprised when told they were doing poorly. They were usually at college at the behest of parents and high school teachers and typically came of fathers of limited educational backgrounds and menial occupations. Many came of rural backgrounds. Psychological tests available on some of these Scholars showed that their interests differed sharply from those of the average college student, tending toward vocational rather than intellectual pursuits. The Farnsworth team suggested that this tendency may be more prevalent among college students in general than is usually supposed. "Probably," they said, "many of

[56]

the students of superior intelligence who do not go to college and who are of so much concern to various commissions studying manpower problems would show similar values to these men."

None of the major causes of Scholar withdrawals reviewed above involved lack of intellectual capacity. As the Farnsworth team reported: "Only rarely did we find in our study that a Scholar left college because of lack of ability. Almost invariably the main reason for leaving centered around a family situation, a cultural consideration, a social difference too wide to be bridged quickly, or a personal attitude that impeded normal development. To alter slightly a phrase coined by one of the advisers, 'they have the intelligence, but it is not at their disposal.'"

A very small minority of the 1951 Scholars (less than 2 per cent) did, however, leave college for the basic reason of lack of intellectual potential. Half of these withdrawals occurred at Shimer, which was the only institution deliberately and on an experimental basis to admit Scholars of average or below-average academic promise. While some of these Scholars succeeded in graduating, none made a distinguished academic record. Several dropped out of the program with varying degrees of discouragement and presumed feelings of inadequacy.

Failures of this nature, the psychiatrists noted, represent the serious fatalities of the program. "Whereas these students might have succeeded in college had they completed secondary school, coming to college shy one year or two of such schooling placed them in a position which doomed them to failure. This group who really wanted a college education were severely traumatized psychologically by their failure. Experience with these students strongly suggests that early admission is applicable only to students with superior intellectual potential."

Summing up, the Farnsworth team found that this 2 per cent of Scholar withdrawals due to lack of intellectual potential constituted the only genuine failures in which early admission had been a major cause—with one other minor exception. At two colleges, a number of failures occurred among Scholars who had entered the program after only two years of high school. "These failures," the Farnsworth team said, "might have been avoided if the students had continued at least one more year in high school." They went on to note, however, that the majority of "tenth-graders" did succeed in the program.

At four of the 11 colleges, the psychiatrists were able to compare their own classification of reasons for individual failures, withdrawals, and transfers with the reasons assigned by the college administration. The accompanying table shows the results of this comparison.

COLLEGES' CLASSIFICATION		PSYCHIATRISTS' CLASSIFICATION	
ACADEMIC FAILURE	9	IMMATURITY	2
		REALISTIC	1
		PSYCHIATRIC DISORDERS	2
		INAPPROPRIATE VALUES	4
FAILURE TO ADJUST	4	IMMATURITY	1
		PSYCHIATRIC DISORDERS	2
		MISCELLANEOUS	1
ENTERED MILITARY SERVICE	1	INAPPROPRIATE VALUES	1
TRANSFERRED	11	REALISTIC REASONS	6
		VOCATIONAL REASONS	5
FINANCIAL	1	REALISTIC	1
HEALTH	2	PSYCHIATRIC DISORDERS	2
MARRIAGE	5	REALISTIC	4
		INAPPROPRIATE VALUES	1
OTHER REASONS	14	UNKNOWN	1
		FOR MISSIONARY WORK	8
		FAMILY MOVED	2
		INAPPROPRIATE VALUES	3

"These comparisons," the Farnsworth team observed, "illustrate the various factors underlying failure to successfully complete college. They suggest the exciting possibility that given better techniques for facilitating emotional growth in the college as a social system, coupled with adequate psychiatric help, the result would be the salvaging for successful college careers of many of the students now failing for various reasons. Especially important would be the development of techniques to impart values for education to those lacking them in sufficient quantity to effect their motivation. Research in this area is badly needed."

A SUMMING UP

ON THE BASIS of the evidence gathered to date on the experience of 1,350 Early Admission Scholars in the 12 participating colleges and universities over a period of five years during which two groups of Scholars have graduated, it is now possible to make much firmer judgments about the results of the experiment—and about the wisdom of early admission in general—than was the case in the summer of 1953, when the Fund published its first preliminary report on the program.

What does the evidence add up to? What were the conclusions of the independent evaluators? How do the Scholars, their Comparison students, their parents, the schools from which they came, and the colleges to which they went, feel about the Early Admission Program in particular and the idea of early admission in general? What are the implications of the results to date for secondary and higher education as a whole?

This final chapter will attempt to answer these questions on the basis of the evidence accumulated thus far.

THE JUDGMENT OF THE SCHOLARS AND COMPARISON STUDENTS

In their senior essays, the 1951 and 1952 Scholars and Comparison students who successfully completed their undergraduate work were asked to express their judgment about the wisdom of early admission on the basis of their own experience and observations.

The Scholars were asked these questions:

In retrospect, how do you feel now about the advantages and disadvantages of having entered college early? On balance, do you think it was profitable in your case?

What advice would you give to a friend of yours who was considering the advisability of entering college at an earlier age than usual?

Do you think the early admission idea should become a **regular** part of the admission policy of American colleges?

The Comparison students were asked this question:

In your opinion, what are the advantages and disadvantages of acceleration? On balance, do you think the idea is wise or unwise? Under what circumstances?

The responses of the Scholars and Comparisons are shown in the table on the following page.

As the table indicates, nearly nine out of ten of the Scholars who were about to graduate said that on balance it had been profitable for them to enter college early, and about eight out of ten Comparisons who were about to graduate expressed themselves as generally favorable toward the early admission idea.

Rather marked changes in attitude are observed when the answers to the four questions by the 1952 Scholars and Comparisons are compared to the responses of the 1951 group. The 1952 Scholars expressed far fewer reservations than their 1951 counterparts about early admission, whether they were asked about it as a personal experience, or in terms of advice to a friend, or in terms of a general policy for American colleges and universities. (One Scholar, in an emphatically affirmative answer to the latter question, wrote: "What I cannot understand is how early admission was once a regular part of American education and then abandoned. As you can imagine, I never miss the name of a great American who went to college early. Cotton Mather entered at twelve. Jonathan Edwards graduated at seventeen. This list could go on and on.")

The 1952 Comparison students also expressed far fewer reservations than their 1951 counterparts about the early admission idea. This increase in the "wholly favorable" category was not accompanied by any comparable shift in the proportion of stu-

THE OVER-ALL JUDGMENT OF SCHOLARS AND
COMPARISONS ABOUT EARLY ADMISSION

RESPONSES BY THE SCHOLARS:	1951 GROUP	1952 GROUP
Was Early Admission profitable in your case?		
YES, VERY MUCH SO	42%	75%
YES, WITH RESERVATIONS	46	15
NEITHER PROFITABLE NOR UNPROFITABLE	7	5
NO, DEFINITELY NOT	4	3
NO RESPONSE	1	2
Would you advise a friend to enter college early?		
YES, DEFINITELY	12%	27%
YES, WITH RESERVATIONS	75	61
ONLY IN EXCEPTIONAL CASES	8	5
NO, DEFINITELY NOT	3	3
NO RESPONSE	2	4
Do you think the Early Admission idea should become a regular part of the admission policy of American colleges?		
YES, DEFINITELY	41%	66%
YES, WITH MINOR MODIFICATIONS	31	15
YES, WITH SEVERE LIMITATIONS	12	16
NO, DEFINITELY NOT	15	2
NO RESPONSE	1	1
RESPONSES BY THE COMPARISONS:	1951 GROUP	1952 GROUP
Do you think acceleration of qualified students is wise?		
YES, DEFINITELY	12%	32%
YES, WITH RESERVATIONS	67	44
ONLY IN EXCEPTIONAL CASES	11	10
NO, DEFINITELY NOT	9	13
NO RESPONSE	1	1

dents expressing wholly unfavorable judgments, except that a much smaller proportion of the 1952 Scholars rejected the idea that early admission become a regular part of the admission policy of American colleges, and a somewhat larger proportion of the 1952 Comparisons were definitely opposed to the acceleration of qualified students. Thus, the responses indicate an even stronger endorsement of the early admission idea by the 1952 Scholars and Comparisons than by their 1951 counterparts.

In their appraisal of the advantages and disadvantages of early admission, the Scholars and Comparison students were virtually in complete agreement. The advantage both cited most frequently was a much greater academic challenge in college than in high school. Fifty-eight per cent of the 1951 Scholars and 82 per cent of the 1952 Scholars cited this as an advantage. The corresponding figures for the Comparison students were 61 per cent and 72 per cent. The views expressed by the Scholars and Comparison students on this point were interesting and revealing. Many of the Scholars said that early admission to college had "rescued" them from an unchallenging high school experience. This view was expressed in several different ways. One Scholar said flatly: "The one year which I missed in high school was, as I was informed by my friends who remained there, a complete waste of time." Another said: "I loved high school because of the extra-curricular activities and my friends, but I was wasting my time academically. College classes were much more of a challenge." A third put it this way: "The [Early Admission Program] picked me up when I still had great interest and ambition, which I feel I would have lost in the next two years. . . . [It] put me into a challenging intellectual atmosphere at precisely the time when I was best equipped to accept it."

The tenor of some of the Scholars' comments on this point suggested that their criticism was aimed not at their high schools but at the "lock step," which frequently keeps able students from entering college when they are ready to, regardless of chronological age or the number of years of prior schooling. This distinction was clearly made by a Scholar from a reputable high school in a large Eastern city who wrote: "I found at college an intellectual challenge and satisfaction which I wanted out of high school work at that time, but which I could not seem to obtain, even though I feel that the high school I attended offered the best high school education that one could receive in ————." It

[63]

also was made by the Scholar who wrote: "High schools are of necessity (and rightly so) geared to the average student, since he forms the majority of our population. Yet if we are to maintain our position of world leadership with any degree of dignity and self-respect at all, we must not neglect the education of those who are our future leaders and who are at present marking time in an educational atmosphere which is not challenging."

Several of the Comparison students made the same point. One wrote: "I have known many accelerated students who would have been seriously frustrated and perhaps permanently damaged by having to spend two additional years in conventional high school." And another, on the basis of personal experience, wrote: "I see no reason, academically, why qualified students should not be able to accelerate their education. From my own experience, I believe that much of the time in the last year of high school is wasted in that the material could either have been taught earlier, or is repeated in college courses.

The next most frequently mentioned advantage on the part of both Scholars and Comparisons was the opportunity for acceleration, which they described in various ways—an earlier start on professional study, an earlier start on a career, an earlier marriage, or an opportunity to finish college before being called up for military service. Several of the students who cited this as an advantage mentioned that the time saved looked less significant from the vantage point of senior year than of freshman year. Pearson concluded that most of these students were more concerned with avoiding wasting time than with saving time.

The Scholars and Comparisons also agreed with respect to the major disadvantages of early admission. The most frequently cited disadvantage was that early admission makes personal and social adjustment to college more difficult. This was cited by 58 per cent of the 1951 Scholars and 65 per cent of the 1952 Scholars. The corresponding figures for the Comparisons were 95 per cent and 83 per cent. Here again the comments of the Scholars were interesting and revealing. Said one:

[64]

On looking back over my past four years here, I am quite glad that I entered college early. However, I honestly believe I am expressing the feeling of one who has 'made the grade' and not the feeling of one who has to do it over again. I sincerely believe, however, that in four years time I have gotten much more out of school than the average student, but it was a tough climb.

Another summed up the matter in these words: "That there are difficulties involved cannot be denied, and many individuals may find the adjustment problems very difficult to overcome, but for the majority I feel these will not be insuperable, or even trying."

Several of the Scholars reported that early admission had actually enhanced their social and emotional development. As one Scholar put it: "From my first moments on campus, college represented a new and exciting experience. I had no difficulty adjusting to this new life, partly because of the sincere interest which the faculty and upperclassmen took in us. . . . The newly acquired self-responsibility was a challenge which stimulated my social and emotional maturation."

The fact that the 1952 Scholars endorsed early admission with far fewer qualifications than the 1951 group, yet cited the personal and emotional adjustment problem as a disadvantage with much greater frequency than the 1951 group appears to be somewhat contradictory. Pearson concluded that the 1952 Scholars, in making an over-all appraisal of their college experience, assigned less weight to this disadvantage than their 1951 counterparts.

The reservations expressed by the Scholars and Comparisons in qualifying their endorsement of the early admission idea were of such a nature as to indicate that they had given the questions thoughtful consideration before answering them. For example, in their answers to the questions about the wisdom of early admission, the reservations dealt not only with the advantages inherent in the program, but also with the kinds of students and the kinds of colleges where the policy was most likely to be successful. In general, both the Scholars and the Comparisons who expressed these reservations felt that the early admission policy should be adopted only by colleges capable of wise selection and proper handling of such students, and should apply only to students who demonstrated exceptional ability and a high degree of social and emotional maturity. One Scholar wrote: "What is really needed . . . is a more effective high school system, but until the answer to this comes, colleges should provide some sort of an escape hatch for the students who are ready to handle advanced work."

After analyzing the Scholars' reservations, Pearson concluded:

The impression one forms in considering these comments is that the important thing is enrichment of the educational program and recognition of individual ability, rather than any particular partiality for the idea of early admission *per se*. These students recognize that the offering of advanced college level courses at secondary schools would probably be limited to a relatively few schools among the total number in the country. To the extent that this is possible, the need for a regular policy of early admission is limited. To the extent that this is not possible, a regular program of early admission is essential. We believe it is clear from these comments that the Scholars look upon early admission as a rather specific exception within the general framework of American education, although from their point of view the exception would be a most important one.

The qualities mentioned by both Scholars and Comparison students as desirable in applicants for early admission included mature appearance, sense of responsibility, emotional stability, self-reliance, adaptability, high motivation for college, and social maturity. Many of the students who pressed for appraisal of these qualities admitted their elusiveness and confessed their inability to describe just how an admission officer could determine their presence or absence in a specific applicant. "Their point," Pearson observed, "is that intellectual readiness for college does not presuppose emotional readiness for college and somehow the latter must be weighed in the balance."

Both Scholars and Comparison students were sharply split on

the relative importance of intellectual readiness and emotional readiness. Some described the ideal student as one who is in the top 5 or 10 per cent of his class scholastically, scores extremely high on college entrance examinations, and is active in extra-curricular activities and sports. There was general agreement that if such an individual were a sophomore or a junior in high school and was frustrated by an unchallenging academic diet, he would be clearly admissible by these high standards. However, it was far less clear from the essays whether favorable early admission action should be taken in the case of a student who was strong intellectually but had a poorer chance of successful college adjustment. One Scholar wrote: "My own prejudice is that only intellectual adequacy to do the work is really relevant; I resent the present attempts of my own university to impose social and intellectual orthodoxy by its admission policy." Another Scholar wrote that at his college "social maturity is much less important than academic preparation." Two other students suggested that the intellectually strong youngster who was not well-adjusted at secondary school was a likely prospect for early admission because he probably would be no worse off in college.

"Quotations such as these," Pearson observed in his report, "contrast quite sharply with the qualities of personal and social maturity which were mentioned quantitatively more often among the essays. A conceivable reconciliation of these somewhat divergent points of view is that intellectual competence is the *sine qua non* for early admission; given this, the final decision should rest on a relative assessment of the applicant's challenge and adjustment at high school and his likely challenge and adjustment at college."

The Scholars and the Comparison students were unanimous in urging a minimum of special treatment for early admission students. Many also urged that college counseling services should be improved. Reports on this aspect were very favorable on some campuses and sharply critical on others. There was a general feeling on the part of most Scholars that a strong counseling system was essential at any college admitting youthful students—not a system uniquely for them, but one which they could share with the rest of the student body.

Finally, the Scholars and the Comparison students stressed the need for a "good fit" between the individual students and the individual college. "This requirement," Pearson noted in his report, "came out in an amusing way in a number of essays where special and fervent pleas were made for confining early admission to small liberal arts colleges, or to large universities, or to highly selective colleges, or to engineering and technical schools. If one were to be guided by the sum total of these suggestions, one would conclude that early admission is a necessary feature at *all* American colleges and universities."

THE VERDICT OF THE INDEPENDENT EVALUATORS
The Pearson Evaluation

The principal conclusions reached by Pearson after his analysis of the senior essays can be summarized as follows:

1. The evidence is that adjustment difficulties were by no means limited to early admission students, although more Scholars than Comparisons reported such difficulties. The conclusion is that early admission was a contributing factor—but not the sole factor—in the existence of adjustment difficulties among the Scholars. However, although the Scholars were faced initially with a greater adjustment problem than the Comparison students, they were able to effect as successful an over-all adjustment as the Comparison students.

"Borrowing from Toynbee, the response to challenge, rather than the challenge itself, becomes a measure of success of the experiment and in these terms we would record our conclusion that the experiment was a success for the students whose essays we have considered in this report."

2. The Scholars' definition of early admission as an exception to general educational practice underscores a concern that

[68]

the able student will be hurt unless special arrangements are made to recognize and develop his ability. From this point of view, early admission or indeed any program of enrichment is viewed as giving the able student the same opportunity as that routinely offered to other students. Similarly, the problem of trying to describe the student for whom early admission would be wise is by no means dissimilar from the problem faced by the admissions officer in attempting to select candidates for regular admission. Finally, the obligation of the college to insure a successful educational experience for the early admission student differs only in detail from the college's obligation toward normal-age students.

"This suggests that the important lesson from the early admission experiment is that the American educational system cannot afford to overlook the individuality of the students with whom it deals. Whether these students are normal age or under-age, or whether they have completed a formal program in secondary school is probably of less importance than their capabilities and aspirations as individuals. The contribution of the schools and the colleges to society is likely to be gauged in terms of how well these are recognized and developed, rather than in terms of formal structures and prescribed programs."

The Farnsworth Evaluation

Dr. Farnsworth and his colleagues, after studying the social and emotional adjustment of the 1951 Scholars, concluded that the Scholars adjusted to campus life as well as their Comparison students and classmates and that the reasons for failures among the Scholars were the same as for college students in general.

They suggested that the following guideposts might be helpful to admissions officers in selecting candidates for early admission, noting that most of them apply equally to the selection of regular freshmen:

a. Such students must be carefully selected on an individual

[69]

basis for the individual college. They should be of the type most apt to benefit from the type of education which the college has to offer.

b. Such students should have above average academic achievement and superior intelligence.

c. Such students, except in unusual cases, should have completed the 11th grade.

d. Personality wise, they should show evidence of emotional maturity at least consistent with their chronological age, good ability in inter-personal relations, and freedom from excessive parental pressure toward early admission. Students who have had frequent changes of schools without similar moves by the family, who come from families with severe discord or who are using college entrance as an escape from serious personal problems are poor risks.

e. Students who have had psychiatric illnesses should have had adequate treatment.

f. Students with characteriological disorders should not be admitted. However, a distinction must be made between misbehavior as representative of a long-standing characteriological disorder and misbehavior as a manifestation of adolescent rebellion. These latter cases, if the difficulties have been overcome, either as a result of the natural maturing process or of psychiatric treatment, should not be excluded.

g. In the selection of students for liberal arts courses, such students should have appropriate educational values, or the capacity to acquire such values.

h. Close scrutiny should be given by large urban universities to students from rural areas.

i. In selection, it is all too easy to err in not admitting the unusually intellectually gifted student or the chronic dissenter who is not "well-rounded." While "well-rounded" students are highly desirable, if this is used as the main criteria for admission these unusual students may be passed over. Such students may make great contributions in the future. As one dean said: "There should be room in our stable for all kinds of horses."

COMMENTS OF SCHOLARS' PARENTS

The colleges and universities participating in the Early Admission Program have not made a systematic effort to determine how the Scholars' parents feel about the program, but two colleges (Goucher and Louisville) conducted special canvasses of the parents of their 1951 Scholars shortly after their graduation. These results, although based on a very small and incomplete statistical sample, tended to confirm the general impression reported by the colleges that the parents on the whole have been favorable toward the program.

In the Goucher survey, 26 of the 27 parents responding said that if they had the choice to make again they would send their daughters to college early. Many of the parental opinions reflected the same balancing of advantages and disadvantages as the Scholar essays. One mother, who said she would again choose early admission for her daughter, remarked nonetheless that the girl had lost contact with her high school classmates and added on the drawback side: "It was, too, a lonely pinnacle of fame in the adolescent community." Another expressed the opinion that entering college early "helped to build up her self-confidence and initiative." Another wrote: "She was made more resourceful and self-reliant; had to think and act independently." And another: "I believe she matured in many ways sooner than if she had completed high school."

In the Louisville survey, 11 of the 12 responses expressed parental approval of the Early Admission Program. The one exception, written by the mother of a Scholar, said in part: "I would never influence a boy or girl again into giving up the last year in high school. . . . [My son] entered engineering school at the age of 16. He needed the chemistry, physics, and math he would have had his last year in High School. He was lost as far as the work was concerned and very unhappy. He had always made good grades. . . . As far as [my son] is concerned the early entry was not right and I've regretted it."

Another Louisville mother, who had two children in the program, wrote: "Since I wasn't sold on the Program when I first heard about it, I'm happy to have the opportunity now to say I'm wholeheartedly in favor of it since our two children have tried it. . . . They both seem happier and better adjusted at the University than they did in High School. They are certainly not either one geniuses but I really believe now that they would have been wasting their time if they had stayed in High School another year. They have even had more social life at the University."

Apart from the Goucher and Louisville surveys, a number of participating institutions have reported their general impressions on the matter of parental attitudes. Utah said it believed that most parents consider going to college early to have been a successful and valuable experience for their children. Fisk reported the reaction of parents to have been "quite favorable." Lafayette said a few of the parents felt that it would have been better for their children to have finished high school, but that most were well-satisfied with the results.

Oberlin reported that the reactions of parents have been difficult to evaluate. It noted that where a Scholar was successful the parents were highly co-operative and pleased but that where it did not work out "the reactions ranged from a mature acceptance to a projection of all the blame on the College." (In a number of these cases, it reported, the Scholars had been strongly encouraged to apply for the Fund scholarships by their parents.)

Wisconsin, on the other hand, reported that the attitude of its Scholars' parents has been "one of the most interesting and heartening aspects of early admission." The parents were pleased and grateful when their sons and daughters did well, Wisconsin added, but "what is more important, when the boys did badly the parents were extremely helpful and co-operative, and to this we probably owe many of the successful recoveries from trouble the Scholars have made. . . . It is interesting that three families have sent two Scholars each."

THE ATTITUDES OF HIGH SCHOOL PRINCIPALS

As with parental attitudes, the participating colleges have not made a systematic effort to gather data about the attitudes of the high schools from which the Scholars were chosen. However, Goucher and Louisville polled the secondary schools from which their 1951 Scholars came, and several of the other colleges have obtained, through correspondence and discussion, a general picture of the reactions of principals and guidance officers.

The available evidence suggests that the character of high school reaction is mixed, ranging from strong approval to strong disapproval, and that to some extent it is in the process of change.

Ten of the 12 participating colleges have reported to the Fund on their experience with high school principals and guidance officers, often in relation to the difficult task of Scholar selection. According to these reports, many of the college officials have encountered considerable resistance to the Early Admission Program. Sometimes this has been vocal. Sometimes, as one college commented, it has not: "The general reaction has been to ignore the plan entirely."

Many teachers and principals in secondary schools have been strongly opposed to the early departure to college of some of their best potential juniors and seniors. As one principal frankly told a college official: "We don't like the idea of the colleges taking our leaders out of high school at the end of the tenth or eleventh grade."

The dean of one of the participating colleges, reporting considerable high school resistance to the Early Admission Program, voiced the opinion that it "is based partially on a genuine concern for the emotional and social development of the individual and a belief that he will be harmed by taking him out of his chronological peers and placing him with his intellectual peers. It may also result partially from the reflection upon the job of the secondary school which is seen in the program."

This dean noted that there appeared to be a marked difference among high schools, depending on the quality of their own instruction. "Those schools which were well-established and doing very good jobs saw this as another indication of the fine work they were doing in having their students qualify for admission after only two or three years with them," he said. "On the other hand, the weaker schools tended to see this as a criticism of the programs which they were performing and a reflection that they were doing so poor a job that an additional year or two with them made little difference in the college success of the student."

Some of the colleges and universities have reported cases of active high school interest in and co-operation with the experiment. For example, one large university reported that the majority of high schools from which its Scholars came were quite enthusiastic and continued to be so, except in the case of a few Scholars who failed to stay. Another university, noting that a few high schools have sent it a large proportion of its Scholars, remarked: "Their views on the program are, of course, colored by the experience of their boys; since they have sent us applicants year after year they presumably approve the plan."

One university said that some principals in its state "have realized early admission could take some burdens from their shoulders, by removing some of the pressure for college preparation of a few students. If, for example, a boy shows potentiality as a scientist, but goes to a school which does not teach mathematics beyond algebra, early admission offers him a way to get his trigonometry, without straining the resources of the school."

A number of the participating institutions reported that high school attitudes, first largely negative, have changed, presumably as a result of experience with early admission, and that there has been a growing acceptance of its possibilities during the last few years.

[74]

Aside from these general observations by the colleges the only direct evidence as to the attitudes of high school principals and guidance officers is afforded by the results of the Goucher and Louisville surveys. The responses to these surveys ranged all the way from strong approval to strong disapproval of early admission, with most of the principals emphasizing that they felt it was wise only for students of exceptional academic ability and social maturity. For example, of the six principals responding to the Louisville survey, two said they approved of the idea, one said the wisdom of early admission depends entirely on the student concerned, another said the idea had both good and bad points, and two disapproved of the idea on the ground that the early admission student misses much by not completing high school. Following are samples of the range of comments:

Students who enter college too young seem to lack social maturity and often are not accepted by the more mature college students. I often wonder how much these students lose by not remaining with their classes and probably taking over positions of leadership during their senior year.

⋅　⋅　⋅

Whether or not it is wise for a high school student to enter college at the end of his junior year depends entirely upon the student concerned. . . . In brief, both the academic progress and the social development of the student must receive equal consideration in making the decision. In our opinion only a relatively small percentage would qualify socially.

⋅　⋅　⋅

I think the [Early Admission] Program has been a distinct service to the students from this school, and I believe I would like to see the program renewed and the selections be made on an individual basis.

The pattern of responses to the Goucher survey was quite similar to that of the Louisville survey. The principals and guidance officers of high schools that had sent the largest number of students into the Early Admission Program tended to be the most favorably disposed toward it. The tenor of the replies suggested that there were two major reasons for this tendency: (1) Since the senior classes in such high schools were generally large, the Scholars were not "missed" as much as they were in small high schools, and (2) since the academic standards of these schools were generally high, the principals tended to be much less sensitive to the implication that the Scholars were offered a much greater academic challenge in college.

The reply of the scholarship counselor in a large Eastern high school that has sent nine students into the Early Admission Program aptly illustrates this tendency. Asked to cite the major advantage of early admission from the student's point of view, she replied: "The student stops 'marking time' and gets on with the real work that he wants to do. If he's mature enough, he gets real satisfaction out of the greater challenge of college work." Asked to cite the major disadvantage of the program from the school's point of view, she wrote: "The school is deprived in the sense that these Early Admission students leave gaps in their class. The school no longer benefits from the stimulation of their superior work and attitudes, and generally from their participation in the extracurricular life of the school." She added, however, that "since our early admission people are so few in number, we feel no significant deprivation; and since we feel that the boys and girls themselves are benefited, we are very happy to see them succeed in college."

Principals of other large Eastern high schools which have sent relatively large numbers of students into the Early Admission Program made similar observations. "Most high schools like to have bright students in their enrollment," wrote the principal of a Massachusetts high school which has furnished eight Scholars. "Occasionally key posts are left vacant (by the departure of early admission students), but they are usually filled by another capable student. Occasionally we find a brilliant student who is bored by his contemporaries; he finds their activities childish. A change in environment could be helpful."

In preparation for this report, the Fund asked each of the participating colleges and universities to study the records of the first two groups of Scholars to graduate and to judge whether early admission had been wise in each individual case. The results of this appraisal were as follows:

OPINION	1951 GROUP	1952 GROUP
WISE	79.6%	76.4%
OPINION DIVIDED	14.6	17.1
UNWISE	5.8	6.5

As the table indicates, the faculty judgment at the participating institutions was that early admission was wise in the case of eight out of ten Scholars in the 1951 group, and in the case of three out of four in the 1952 group. (It must be remembered that the judgments covered only those Scholars who had survived through senior year.)

The Fund also asked the participating institutions to appraise their experience under the Early Admission Program, and invited them to comment on the broad implications of the results to date for American secondary and higher education as a whole.

Excerpts from their reports follow:

The University of Chicago

The Chicago campus made adjustment easier in that there were so many students of the same age as the Scholars. For approximately ten years prior to the start of the Early Admission Program, the University of Chicago had admitted students to the College who had completed no more than two years of high school. The Early Admission Scholars who entered in 1951 and in each succeeding year were only a fraction of the total number of entering students who had not graduated from high school. I think, too, the curriculum made adjustment easier. The curriculum at the University of Chicago is arranged so as to allow each student to proceed at his own best pace. But Chicago is a large metropolitan University, and for many reasons a large university is not the ideal home for everyone, and I suppose the youth of some Scholars makes adjustment to a metropolitan campus difficult. The student body at Chicago is divided between commuting students and resident students. There is not the homogeneity in campus life that many colleges can achieve. This may have been one factor affecting the younger students, although the large number of early entrants at Chicago has made possible the development of athletics and extra-curricular activities which fit their needs.

Despite all of these factors, however, I am confident that the overwhelming majority of the Scholars (and other early entrants) at Chicago have adjusted well, that they have been glad that they entered college early, and have found an intellectual stimulation from college that they would not have found during the corresponding years of high school. I see no reason to believe that the intellectual stimulation for this majority was achieved at the expense of social maladjustment. They have more than held their own in the social life of the campus.

Columbia College

When, in the spring of 1955, the Columbia College faculty instructed the committee responsible for admissions that up to 25 early admission candidates might be admitted within any one year, the action clearly had a double significance. It represents, in the first place, a formal acceptance of the desirability and practicability of early admission for qualified candidates. But the limitation of the number to be admitted reflects the special situation of Columbia College. New York City and the Metropolitan Area offer a rich source of student talent. We attract boys from this region as a national college which can be reached by subway. However, most of our applicants for early admission live in New York City. Our status as a national college is maintained by our capacity to draw students from beyond the confines of the metropolis. Simply adding to our representation from New York and its immediate environs will undercut the very basis on which we appeal to the highly talented youths within that area. Moreover, an increase in our New York City contingent would distort our pre-professional balance, because a high proportion of New York City applicants for early admission are pre-medical students of whom we already have as high a proportion as we can handle without damage to our liberal arts program.

If it were possible to secure a large number of equally able early admission candidates from the country at large, Columbia would benefit greatly. But the widespread announcement of the early admission opportunity in earlier years produced very few candidates from good schools in other urban centers, and it has been our experience that the boy from a small school, remote from an urban center, needs, when he comes to Columbia, whatever assurance and maturity his final year in high school or a year's additional growth can bestow. Our National Scholarship Program provides a direct answer to our problem here.

This is an immediate and practical response, dictated by our faith in the value of the kind of work we can do with the able students, diversified as to geographical origin and background, who come to us now. Much of the value of institutions of higher learning lies in their *distinctive* capacities to contribute to the national life.

But early admission, considered independently, poses no discernible threat to such distinctive contributions as a variety of institutions afford, and it promises to fulfill the hope of those who have tried it: to achieve a closer and more efficacious relation between the school and the college. This, at least, is our experience, and we are happy to report that Columbia and the youngsters who came early to the feast have both profited.

Fisk University

It has been made clear that the distinctly superior student coming out of the tenth or eleventh grade can succeed well with college freshman work provided the student also has good motivation and reasonable emotional maturity. The distinctly superior academic capacity of the Ford Scholars has emphasized the fact that the College needs freshman courses at different levels to meet the ability and preparation of a wide variety of students. (This variety is bound to persist in any college which does not require entrance examinations either in aptitude or achievement.)

The best of the Scholars have done so well academically that they have challenged others to keep pace with them and have challenged instructors to raise their expectation in certain courses. The leadership of the Scholars in various extra-curricular activities has stimulated these organizations very distinctly . . .

. . . In connection with considering an appropriate curriculum for Ford Scholars, we have reviewed and rebuilt our whole general education program for freshmen and sophomores.

Goucher College

It is not easy to draw conclusions from an educational project that

[79]

has been as wide flung in its implications as the Early Admission Program, but with five years of experience in it we would like to make two points: the first touching on the merits of early admission *vis-à-vis* admission with advanced standing, with a side look at the much discussed question of the social adjustment of those entering as early admission students; the second on qualitative differences that have been revealed in the four early admission groups we admitted with the financial aid of The Fund for the Advancement of Education.

In our opinion it is very doubtful that the so-called enrichment programs in high school can meet as well as a college or university the total intellectual and social needs of patently superior students. We say this not out of a partisan feeling for early admission but out of a realization that the superior student should feel a gravitational pull not in one or two courses alone but in all the student's educational and social pursuits. This absolute need we believe can be met by very few, if any, high schools in the country.

If we are asked by what signs we may know the superior student we would point to an outstanding educational record in high school supported by College Board aptitude and achievement scores in the 600's preferably, though some scores in the high 500's would be acceptable. These objective data we would want fortified by the recommendations of the high school principals.

Queried about social adjustment and maturity (two very different concepts, not necessarily reconcilable) we would reply that an early admission student should give evidence at entrance to college of the capacity to catch up in the space of two years with those who will be her college classmates. If the student is intellectually ready for college we think she should be admitted even if there will be some periods of social and personal strain ahead of her (and we would believe that in almost every case they would be inevitable). We are convinced that as these stem from superior ability and differentness, the early admission student has a better chance of meeting them more happily in a setting where the intellectual is not considered a "freak" or a young Einstein. We believe that the ampler ether of college or university will serve to help the student with superior endowment to wait on the maturing processes of time without vulgarizing herself by seeking mere conformity or by denigrating her intellectual resources by calling them "compensations." In other words we believe that social maturity can be sooner and better achieved by the superior student with less waste of spirit in college than in high school.

[80]

As to the best time of entrance to college for the patently superior student we are at this point almost inclined to say the end of the tenth year, though there is a possible danger of shortchanging the student in her preparation for college work in the sciences and mathematics. Our inclination toward the tenth year has been influenced by the facts (1) that some of our tenth year students have been among our best; (2) that a lack of intellectual challenge may result in a dulling of intellectual interests and/or in a failure of habits of industry, which failure spread over two years in high school blights performance and attitude in college; and (3) that the longer a student is entrenched in the extra-curricular life of her high school the harder it is to extricate herself without cries of woe from those who are more interested in the extra dividends paid by high office in the senior year than by the intellectual and, we believe, total achievement of the student in question.

The second observation we wish to make is one which bears on the question of qualitative differences within early admission groups. We believe that after five years of experience in selecting early admission students for admission we are better informed about what constitutes what we call, reverting to an earlier terminology, a "true Ford," or an early admission student whom we would define as one who by the end of the first or second year of college has (1) made a good beginning in self-knowledge (and discipline); (2) revealed purposefulness in planning and execution; and, above everything else, (3) shown a sensitivity to form and plan and order, this last in the high sense of Schiller's *"heilige Ordnung."*

But even developing expertness in selection has not increased our yield of "true Fords" in each class. Always they number about one-third of the group. What makes the difference between those equally endowed in mental acuity is a question we cannot yet answer, if we ever can. But henceforth we shall be studying subjective classifications, seeing how far they correlate with objective data.

Using the three criteria mentioned above in the qualitative description of a "true Ford" we think we can divide by the end of the *third* year each early admission class into three groups: the first in patent possession of those qualities; the second group definitely above average in their grasp of their value but not ("yet" might be added parenthetically since self-education will be carried on beyond graduation) in possession of them; the third group, average in their ability to see order or to give form and order to their plans and ideas. It should be recognized that these three classifications are *not* based on such objective data as grade point averages or College Board scores, but depend ultimately on our judgment of the student in the light of value criteria. But the classifications can yield interesting objective data. We intend to study and report on our findings next year.

Lafayette College

Lafayette College feels that the Early Admission Program has been a success. The record of the achievement of the Ford scholars in academic work and extra activities is an excellent one. For this reason, the College plans to continue to admit qualified students even though they have not been graduated from secondary school.

Even though the groups to be admitted to college under this program will probably never be large, the Early Admission Program does offer an excellent opportunity to the young man who is more mature intellectually, socially, and emotionally than his age group. If he is desirous of accelerating his educational program, it is evident that he can do so without losing any of the advantages of college life.

University of Louisville

It is the opinion of all persons concerned with the Early Admission Program that it has been most successful. The University of Louisville has admitted students to its College of Arts and Sciences after three years of high school since 1934, and that program will continue. There is no definite arrangement for financial assistance to such students except that which the Student Aid Committee is able to give them if they need help.

. . . .

From our experience with the Early Admission Program during the past four years, we have learned that a good student, after three years of high school, can do a good job in college if he is well adjusted emotionally and socially before he comes.

. . . .

The program has caused us to examine the aspects of our program that affect all students. We are now trying to locate within our own students the superior student and to do more for him. . . . It is our hope that much more can be done to give more public recognition to these superior students and also to enrich our academic offerings to them.

. . . .

One of the main implications of the Program for secondary and higher education generally is that more should be done to identify the superior student and to enrich his educational program.

Oberlin College

There still seem to be some real difficulties in attracting and selecting appropriate students for early admission. There is still considerable resistance on the part of many secondary school educators to the early admission principle. This is based partially on a genuine concern for the emotional and social development of the individual and a belief that he will be harmed by taking him out of his chronological peers and placing him with his intellectual peers. It may also result partially from the reflection upon the job of the secondary school which is seen in the Program. Still a third difficulty in the way of attracting the proper students for the Program lies in the fact that the schools which have given most publicity to the Early Admission Program have been the better high schools and preparatory schools which are doing a relatively effective job in their own right. The student of superior ability who is stuck in a second-rate high school may not even hear about the Early Admission Program, yet he is the person who could benefit most from being selected for such advancement.

. . . .

The results of the Early Admission Program at Oberlin were carefully reviewed during this past year and the faculty took action this spring to continue to admit students who had a minimum of two years of high school work and who, in the opinion of the Director of Admissions, were ready for admission to college. There are, of course, broad differences of opinion about the advisability of such a program among our faculty, but enough of them felt it had been sufficiently successful to continue on the above mentioned basis. No special scholarship program will be offered for these early admission students who may be admitted in succeeding classes, but they will be permitted to compete for any of the regular Admissions Office scholarships open to four-year students.

. . . .

The general success of the Early Admission Program certainly suggests the lack of adequate provision in the vast majority of our secondary schools and colleges for the truly superior student. It would appear that there is a considerable number of students who are marking time in many high schools during their last one or two

[83]

years there. If they are gaining much educationally, it may very possibly be because they are educating themselves as a result of their intellectual curiosity rather than because of anything the school itself is doing to educate them. At the same time it would appear that many students coming out of four years of experience in good secondary schools may very well be marking time educationally in the first year or two spent in college. The basic implication I see in the results of the Early Admission Program is the tremendous need for better integration of secondary and college education and more provision for the education of the superior student at both of these levels.

Shimer College

Shimer feels that the Early Admission Program has very real value for the pre-professional student. Faced with a long program of specialization, the early entrant finds that his program is accelerated to such an extent that he may begin his professional training at least a year earlier than the student who finishes high school before entering college.

.   .   .   .

In some measure, the admission program at Shimer will undergo a slight change as a result of this recent experience. Probably the percentage of students under the Early Admission Program will be somewhat decreased, with an even greater emphasis on the student who is particularly qualified, both in terms of academic preparation and social adjustment. The administration and faculty of the College believe strongly in the Early Admission Program, and every effort is being made by the College to secure financial underwriting for early entrant scholarships.

.   .   .   .

While it is doubtful that this program with its limitation in numbers will specifically affect the structure of the American education system, it would seem that there is adequate evidence that the qualified student can perform successfully in college without the usually prescribed sixteen Carnegie units. This evidence should lead to some revision of admission policy on the part of many colleges and universities since it is evident that neither the sixteen units are absolutely required, nor are specifically required high school course groupings absolutely necessary.

[84]

In summary, those of us who have been close to the Early Admission Program at the University of Utah view the program after four years as a successful and valuable experience. We believe, moreover, that this attitude is shared by a great majority of the Scholars and their parents and by a growing number of high school administrators and teachers.

.   .   .   .

We believe the problem of the abler student to be especially serious and difficult of solution in situations like ours, where State law requires all young people to remain in school until they are eighteen or have been graduated from high school and where a high school diploma, with rare exceptions, is a guarantee of university or college admission. It will become increasingly acute in the next decade with the great increase in students entering our gates. However, it seems to us that the University of Utah with its geographically homogeneous population and its potentially close relationships with the schools from which its students come has a very special opportunity and challenge to do something about it.

Our special situation is but one illustration of the many striking differences among our higher institutions, even among the small number of institutions engaged in the early admission experiment, and points out again that there are no simple answers, let alone a single one, to the problem. However, we believe that there are some general implications from our experience for secondary and higher education and for the Fund in planning its future program. We believe that, theoretically at least, admission with advanced standing would be sounder psychologically for the students than early admission and better in its effect upon the high schools. However, only a handful of schools in our State could possibly carry out such a program, and even in them the problems of staff and finance would be very great. The same lack of resources would confront any major effort in behalf of the individual student such as is carried on in the Portland experiment.

Under our circumstances the early admission program was the best immediate answer. It caused the least disruption; except for the scholarships it cost relatively little; and, as we have seen, it has been quite successful. However, it has serious disadvantages. It inevitably

[85]

serves too few of the students we are trying to help; attractive scholarships play too great a part; the high schools are too little involved; and the ultimate effect upon secondary education is negative rather than positive.

This last is probably the most important point. To the student, the parents, the schools themselves, and the public the inference is inescapable that the senior year in high school is a waste of time. For the student, high school education is a truncated rather than an integrated and completed educational and social experience. The tendency for the school, if it is not simply hostile to the whole business, is to feel that it can do nothing special for the abler student and to pass the responsibility on to the college or the university.

Yet both acceleration and enrichment are desirable and even necessary for our better students. . . . One way to achieve the desired results for all might be for the schools to reconsider a plan once in effect, if not now, in certain systems. This plan provided a faster track for the better students, which began in the seventh grade, eliminated the eighth grade, and permitted them to complete a full senior high school program a year early and in sufficient numbers to retain the values of their peer group. If such acceleration were combined with a rich program of basic academic subjects and if the higher institutions were alert and flexible in the handling of the students when they entered, great good might result. The success of any such program would depend ultimately upon adequate counseling based upon a conviction that individual differences make it as democratic and vital to identify and serve the needs of the student of high ability as the student of low.

University of Wisconsin

The question is often asked, "Should the colleges make a general practice of accepting students who have not finished high school?" or its converse, "Should high schools make a general practice of recommending such students to college?" As they stand, these questions receive a qualified negative answer; our experience shows that early admission demands what appears to be an unusual combination of intellectual and social precocity. It is probably not as rare as it seems on the surface; there may be as many as a fifth of most high school classes who could make the grade. But the vast majority of these would probably gain nothing by early admission, and the principals have undoubtedly been wise when they have hesitated in recommend-

[86]

ing many applicants. On the other hand, there are a few boys who have almost certainly gained more from college than they would have from their last years of high school; a wise principal will be able to pick them, and the ideal situation would be that in which the original suggestion came from the school rather than the individual student or his parents. Unfortunately, not every teacher's judgment is infallible, and the method of selection remains a problem.

As they make their decision, they must take into account the matter of finances. The Scholars have had much less pressure on them to earn part of their way than the majority of their fellow students, and this has undoubtedly been an important factor in their success: at least two who have been dropped failed partly because they were trying too hard to earn money on the side. This is not easy for boys of sixteen, for even in the summer they cannot get jobs at respectable pay. For the past two years the stipends for freshman and sophomore Scholars have averaged $540, of which $500 must be used for tuition and fees by out-of-state students; Wisconsin students pay $180. About a fifth of the students accepted have decided that they could not afford to take advantage of the offer. We feel that any early admission student must be assured of sufficient financial support, either from his family or from scholarship aid, before he accepts the award; he cannot rely on being able to pay his own way until his junior year. After that, of course, he is in the same position as any other student.

With all these restrictions, intellectual, moral, and financial, it is clear that early admission is only advisable for a tiny proportion of high school students, and that it accents more problems than it answers. It has long been patent that most high schools cannot really push their ablest students, and that the students consequently are apt to lose their enthusiasm in the boredom of waiting for their fellows to catch up with them. Two of the Scholars, one in each of the first two classes, compressed high school and college into five years and graduated as members of Phi Beta Kappa; the very fact that this is possible points to the waste of time which must often take place. Some of this waste can, perhaps, be avoided; some schools have honor classes, a few are able to have a general standard high enough to keep all but the very ablest stimulated. Some duplication of courses might be avoided, especially in the sciences and American history; many colleges allow a student to take work at an advanced level in certain fields if he can show he is qualified, and good high school teaching should certainly be encouraged in this way. Even if the number of years of school and college is not reduced, there is certainly a need to keep able students working at full capacity. Early admission can do this for a few, but the solution on a large scale must be sought elsewhere.

In sum, early admission has offered a partial solution to the problems of getting the best from able students and of shortening the cruelly long period necessary for technical training. The solution is only partial because probably only a very few students have the balanced development of intelligence, personality, and *savoir faire* it demands. At Wisconsin it seems to have been generally quite successful, and it could be more so if we had better techniques of selection and enough Scholars so that each one would not feel himself to be something quite apart from the ordinary university student. It will probably always be expensive, and there will always be some failures among the Scholars who embark on this course, but the benefit to the successful is very great.

Yale University

It seems to be true that the Yale environment presented a more difficult adjustment problem to the Scholars than did many of the other colleges in which the early admissions Scholars matriculated. The fact that almost all of the boys were from high schools and many from relatively small schools no doubt made more difficult their adjustment to a fairly sizeable campus in an urban center.

. . . .

. . . the 1952 group seems to have made a more successful adjustment to the Yale environment. This can be attributed both to the fact that the adjustment factor was more in our minds when we admitted the second group, and perhaps too, to the fact that they were in no way isolated during their first year on our campus as were the 1951 Scholars.

. . . .

Yale University felt that it had received maximum benefit from the Early Admission Program as sponsored by the Fund for the Advancement of Education after its first two years of participation. From that experience the University decided to adopt as part of its Admissions program measures which would give qualified students desiring to enter college from their Junior year in school a chance to do so. To quote from the catalogue of Yale for 1955–56: "Although an applicant is normally expected to have completed four years of secondary school work for entrance, an exception will occasionally be made for a candidate of unusual promise and maturity who has completed three years." No particular scholarship arrangements are made for this group other than those made for all applicants for financial aid. The University does not make a special effort to find and encourage Early Admission applications.

.   .   .   .

Yale feels that early admissions should be part of the policy of every college and university. It does not, however, feel that a specific number of places should be reserved for early admission candidates in each class, nor that a university such as our own should make special effort to attract such Scholars other than having as its policy the admission of those duly qualified.

THE FUTURE OF EARLY ADMISSION

In *Bridging the Gap Between School and College,* the Fund said that the preliminary results of the Early Admission Program were "decidedly encouraging." On the basis of the evidence presented in this report, it now feels that the results to date have been impressive.

Although the period of Fund support has ended, 11 of the 12 colleges participating in the experiment have incorporated the early admission idea into their regular admissions policy. (Wisconsin has not yet taken any action on the matter.) At least one of the colleges—Goucher—has set up a special scholarship program for early admission students. At the other colleges, early admission students are permitted to compete for scholarship aid on equal terms with other entering freshmen.

There are some indications that the early admission idea is gaining wider acceptance. The College Entrance Examination Board reports that 29 of its 169 member colleges had early admission programs in the academic year 1955–56. Only six of these were participants in the Fund-supported experiment. It is interesting to note that 27 of the 29 also had programs of advanced placement, thus providing able high school students two

[89]

different kinds of opportunity for college-level work before graduation.

It is much too early yet to predict the future of the early admission idea, but the evidence in this report clearly indicates that under the proper circumstances it represents a promising approach to the problem of enabling the very best students to realize their full potential. The risks of entering college early have been the subject of much popular concern, and properly so. But too little thought has been given to the risks run by an able student in an unchallenging environment in *not* entering college early. As one of the Scholars wrote in his senior essay: "There is some danger that a young student's talents will be harmed by being thrust among older students who do not accept him. But the greater danger is that he will be allowed to stagnate in secondary school and will arrive in college lacking imagination and ambition, these having been 'educated' out of him. The harm to him and society is great."

Richard Pearson observed in his report that "the important lesson from the Early Admission experiment is that the American educational system cannot afford to overlook the individuality of the students with whom it deals. Whether these students are normal age or underage, or whether they have completed a formal program in secondary school is probably of less importance than their capabilities and aspirations as individuals. The contribution of the schools and colleges to society is likely to be gauged in terms of how well these are recognized and developed, rather than in terms of formal structures and prescribed programs."

Yet there is some danger that in the decades ahead, when American colleges and universities become engrossed in the problems attendant upon steeply rising enrollments, the capabilities and aspirations of the "unusual" student are likely to be neglected. College admissions officers, confronted with the happy prospect of having many more applications for admission than there are places to be filled, may well tend to "play it safe" and to avoid the risks involved in admitting unconventional students, particularly those who are younger than most and who have had a less-than-normal high school preparation. It will be all too easy to say, "We'll get them next year anyhow, and another year in high school won't hurt them." But the evidence clearly indicates that the superior student *can* be hurt by being detained in an intellectual environment he has outgrown. As one Scholar wrote in his senior essay: "I don't advocate anything so radical as a society composed exclusively of eggheads, but it seems downright cruel to force a gifted child to suffer needless years of boredom (and boredom can be suffering, I know) when he can have an opportunity (whether or not he utilizes it is obviously up to him) to meet some fine minds on a college faculty which might be able to salvage at least part of his intellectual potential before the habit of mental laziness has completely encrusted him."

The notion that the superior student does not need special attention because he is bright enough to look out for himself is still widely prevalent, but an increasing number of thoughtful educators and laymen have begun to challenge it and the assumption that regardless of ability and energy each student must move with his chronological age group through eight years of elementary school, four years of high school, and four years of college. Coupled with this has been a critical re-examination of the meaning of educational equality in a democratic society—a questioning as to whether it means equal amounts of education for all or equal opportunity for each individual to develop his talents as fully and freely as possible.

There is also a growing awareness that the health and vigor of our society—and indeed even its very life—depend on making the most of all the capacities of all of our people. And it has become increasingly clear that if we are to make the most of these capacities, we must not fail to provide for the fullest possible development of our ablest young people. The Fund for the Advancement of Education believes that the Early Admission experiment has clearly demonstrated its promise as a means to that end.

APPENDIX

TABLE 1

NUMBER OF SCHOLARS AND COMPARISON STUDENTS
BY COLLEGE AND YEAR OF ENTRANCE

COLLEGE	1951 GROUP		1952 GROUP		1953 GROUP		1954 GROUP		TOTAL	
	S	C	S	C	S	C	S	C	S	C
CHICAGO	60	57	54	54	23	23	21	21	158	155
COLUMBIA	51	46	46	44	24	24	22	22	143	136
FISK	28	28	36	30	31	30	27	27	122	115
GOUCHER	19	19	22	27	15	15	17	17	73	78
LAFAYETTE	30	40	23	29	14	19	0	0	67	88
LOUISVILLE	29	24	29	26	19	17	20	20	97	87
MOREHOUSE	—	—	29	35	28	38	24	31	81	104
OBERLIN	25	30	29	37	17	23	16	21	87	111
SHIMER	34	—	32	—	29	—	30	—	125	—
UTAH	40	52	45	80	38	38	30	30	153	200
WISCONSIN	52	68	48	52	13	21	26	34	139	175
YALE	52	51	47	58	3	15	3	0	105	124
TOTAL	420	415	440	472	254	263	236	223	1,350	1,373

TABLE II

DISTRIBUTION OF SCHOLARS BY HOME STATE

STATE	1951 GROUP	1952 GROUP	1953 GROUP	1954 GROUP	TOTAL
ALABAMA	4	7	6	6	23
ARIZONA	1	2	1	1	5
ARKANSAS	0	4	2	0	6
CALIFORNIA	13	9	4	2	28
COLORADO	2	3	1	1	7
CONNECTICUT	10	7	2	1	20
DELAWARE	0	1	0	0	1
FLORIDA	2	7	6	3	18
GEORGIA	4	16	9	7	36
IDAHO	0	1	1	0	2
ILLINOIS	43	27	22	13	105
INDIANA	3	8	3	3	17
IOWA	2	2	2	1	7
KANSAS	2	1	0	0	3
KENTUCKY	28	16	22	21	87
LOUISIANA	0	3	0	5	8
MAINE	1	1	0	2	4
MARYLAND	7	11	5	5	28
MASSACHUSETTS	12	8	2	2	24
MICHIGAN	10	6	4	3	23
MINNESOTA	1	4	0	4	9
MISSISSIPPI	0	2	0	2	4
MISSOURI	0	6	0	0	6
MONTANA	1	1	0	0	2
NEBRASKA	3	1	0	0	4
NEVADA	0	0	0	0	0
NEW HAMPSHIRE	1	1	2	0	4
NEW JERSEY	35	22	8	7	72
NEW MEXICO	0	1	0	0	1
NEW YORK	111	141	54	62	368
NORTH CAROLINA	0	3	6	10	19
NORTH DAKOTA	1	0	0	1	2
OHIO	20	9	9	5	43
OKLAHOMA	2	0	1	1	4
OREGON	2	3	2	0	7
PENNSYLVANIA	30	18	6	8	62
RHODE ISLAND	2	1	0	1	4
SOUTH CAROLINA	3	1	1	2	7
SOUTH DAKOTA	0	0	0	0	0
TENNESSEE	4	9	6	11	30
TEXAS	1	8	6	4	19
UTAH	41	41	39	29	150
VERMONT	2	1	2	0	5
VIRGINIA	8	11	6	1	26
WASHINGTON	1	2	1	2	6
WEST VIRGINIA	0	3	0	0	3
WISCONSIN	4	3	9	9	25
WYOMING	0	0	0	0	0
DISTRICT OF COLUMBIA	3	8	4	1	16
FOREIGN	0	0	0	0	0
TOTAL	420	440	254	236	1,350

TABLE III

WHAT THE SCHOLARS WERE LIKE*

| | | ANNUAL GROUPS | | | | TOTAL | |
		1951	1952	1953	1954	NO.	%
SEX	Male	348	363	165	148	1,024	75.9
	Female	72	77	89	88	326	24.1
AGE AT	Under 16	110	156	72	58	396	29.3
ENTRANCE	16	263	230	137	131	761	56.4
	17 and over	47	54	45	47	193	14.3
YEARS OF SCHOOLING	Ten	174	202	100	90	566	41.9
COMPLETED	Eleven	209	193	144	142	688	51.0
	Twelve	37	45	10	4	96	7.1
SIZE OF HOME	Large city						
COMMUNITY	(over 100,000)	122	170	111	108	511	48.7
	Suburb of						
	large city	43	39	20	32	134	12.7
	Medium size city						
	(10,000–100,000)	47	67	48	29	191	18.2
	Small town						
	(2,500–10,000)	28	35	26	20	109	10.4
	Rural area						
	(under 2,500)	27	25	20	33	105	10.0
	No data	153	104	29	14	300	
TYPE OF	City public	191	247	175	155	768	73.2
SECONDARY SCHOOL	Suburban public	31	31	20	34	116	11.1
ATTENDED	Rural public	18	23	14	14	69	6.5
	Private	27	36	13	20	96	9.2
	No data	153	103	32	13	301	
SIZE OF	Under 50	35	39	23	30	127	12.7
SENIOR CLASS	50–99	23	40	30	38	131	13.1
AT SECONDARY	100–199	36	52	42	38	168	16.8
SCHOOL	200–499	94	101	67	49	311	31.1
	500 or over	66	86	51	60	263	26.3
	No data	166	122	41	21	350	
FAMILY	Under $2,000	5	5	8	7	25	3.5
INCOME	$2,000–4,999	56	71	44	50	221	30.5
	$5,000–8,999	87	87	60	67	301	41.6
	$9,000 or over	63	53	31	30	177	24.4
	No data	209	224	111	82	626	

* Percentages are based on number of Scholars for whom data were available.

TABLE III *continued*

WHAT THE SCHOLARS WERE LIKE

		ANNUAL GROUPS				TOTAL	
		1951	1952	1953	1954	NO.	%
OCCUPATION OF	Professional	143	139	75	82	439	38.1
BREADWINNING	Business	118	128	69	59	374	32.5
PARENT	Laborer	57	80	60	56	253	22.0
	Government	14	24	11	9	58	5.1
	Farmer	3	11	3	9	26	2.3
	No data	85	58	36	21	200	
HIGHEST LEVEL	Less than 12 years	46	59	39	42	186	18.5
OF SCHOOLING	Graduated high						
COMPLETED BY	school	39	46	23	33	141	14.0
SCHOLARS' FATHERS	Attended college	32	49	47	34	162	16.1
	Graduated college	35	48	36	29	148	14.7
	Attended						
	graduate school	18	8	16	9	51	5.1
	Master's degree	31	33	14	21	99	9.9
	Higher degree	56	73	37	51	217	21.6
	No data	163	124	42	17	346	
FIRST CHOICE OF	Humanities	46	39	25	18	128	10.5
MAJOR FIELD	Social Science	78	56	31	31	196	16.1
OF STUDY	Science or						
	engineering	175	220	121	104	620	50.8
	Education	6	8	2	16	32	2.6
	Business	11	8	3	5	27	2.2
	Agriculture	1	1	5	0	7	.6
	Other	1	1	4	35	41	3.4
	Undecided	35	80	39	14	168	13.8
	No data	67	27	24	13	131	
FIRST CHOICE	Teaching	33	20	22	31	106	9.4
OF FUTURE	Law	20	23	6	8	57	5.0
OCCUPATIONAL	Medicine	51	82	48	54	235	20.8
FIELD	Science or						
	engineering	77	88	38	46	249	21.9
	Business	14	7	3	5	29	2.6
	Agriculture	1	3	0	0	4	.4
	Other	46	34	18	48	146	12.9
	Undecided	96	121	57	32	306	27.0
	No data	82	62	62	12	218	

TABLE IV

ACADEMIC PREPARATION OF SCHOLARS AND COMPARISON STUDENTS

A. Fields in Which Scholars and Comparison Students Felt Handicapped Initially by Faulty or Insufficient Preparation in Secondary School

FIELDS OF REPORTED HANDICAP	1951 GROUP				1952 GROUP				1953 GROUP				1954 GROUP			
	SCHOLARS		COMPAR.		SCHOLARS		COMPAR.		SCHOLARS		COMPAR.		SCHOLARS		COMPAR.	
	N	%	N	%	N	%	N	%	N	%	N	%	N	%	N	%
NONE	189	53.8	195	59.4	200	48.5	218	50.6	93	41.7	86	41.3	92	41.6	73	39.2
ENGLISH COMPOSITION	43	12.3	32	9.8	61	14.8	64	14.8	48	21.5	43	20.7	23	10.4	18	9.7
ENGLISH LITERATURE	8	2.3	2	.6	9	2.2	8	1.9	2	.9	3	1.4	9	4.1	4	2.2
SOCIAL SCIENCE	15	4.3	11	3.4	37	9.0	26	6.0	13	5.8	8	3.8	11	5.0	14	7.5
NATURAL SCIENCE	26	7.4	23	7.0	35	8.5	43	10.0	18	8.1	17	8.2	11	5.0	9	4.8
MATHEMATICS	49	14.0	38	11.6	43	10.4	35	8.1	22	9.9	21	10.1	46	20.8	27	14.5
FOREIGN LANGUAGE	8	2.3	16	4.9	14	3.4	18	4.2	11	4.9	9	4.3	19	8.6	27	14.5
OTHER FIELDS	13	3.7	11	3.4	13	3.2	19	4.4	16	7.2	21	10.1	10	4.5	14	7.5
TOTAL	351		328		412		431		223		208		221		186	

NOTE: Reports were not available for the following groups:
1953—Yale: Comparison students; Louisville: no data received.
1954—Yale: Comparison students; Lafayette: no new cases in study in 1954.
No Comparison students at Shimer during entire program.

TABLE IV *continued*

ACADEMIC PREPARATION OF SCHOLARS AND COMPARISON STUDENTS

B. Gaps or Omissions in Secondary School Preparation
Reported by College as Remaining at End of Second Year

FIELD	1951 GROUP SCHOLARS N	%	COMPAR. N	%	1952 GROUP SCHOLARS N	%	COMPAR. N	%	1953 GROUP SCHOLARS N	%	COMPAR. N	%	1954 GROUP SCHOLARS N	%	COMPAR. N	%
NONE	231	92.8	189	96.9	227	87.6	186	97.4	150	90.4	121	93.1	147	87.0	131	85.1
ENGLISH COMPOSITION	3	1.2	1	.5	2	.8	1	.5	3	1.8	4	3.1	3	1.8		
ENGLISH LITERATURE					11	4.2			1	.6			—	—	3	1.9
SOCIAL SCIENCE	10	4.0	1	.5	5	1.9			1	.6			2	1.2		
NATURAL SCIENCE					9	3.5	2	1.0	1	.6			2	1.2	1	.6
MATHEMATICS	4	1.6	1	.5	2	.8	1	.5	2	1.2	1	.8	1	.6	3	1.9
FOREIGN LANGUAGE	1	.4	3	1.5	3	1.2	1	.5	8	4.8	4	3.1	14	8.3	16	10.4
TOTAL	249		195		259		191		166		130		169		154	

NOTE: Reports were not available for the following groups:
1951 – Morehouse: not in study in 1951.
1952 – Louisville: no data received.
No Comparison students at Shimer during entire program.

TABLE V

ACADEMIC PERFORMANCE OF SCHOLARS
AND COMPARISON STUDENTS

A. *Percentile Rank in Class*

1951 GROUP · FRESHMAN YEAR

PERCENTILE RANK IN CLASS	CHICAGO S	C	COLUMBIA S	C	FISK S	C	GOUCHER S	C	LAFAYETTE S	C	LOUISVILLE S	C	MOREHOUSE S C
80–99	*		18	12	**		8	3	12	13	13	8	Not in
60–79			11	12			6	4	3	12	3	5	program
40–59			12	8			2	2	8	5	3	2	in
20–39			3	9			2	1	3	5	6	3	1951
0–19			3	5			1	2	1				
Number of Students Ranked			47	46			19	12	27	35	25	18	

1951 GROUP · SOPHOMORE YEAR

PERCENTILE RANK IN CLASS	CHICAGO S	C	COLUMBIA S	C	FISK S	C	GOUCHER S	C	LAFAYETTE S	C	LOUISVILLE S	C	MOREHOUSE S C
80–99	34	8	17	9	**		10	4	15	18	13	7	Not in
60–79	7	13	13	12			1	2	10	3	4	4	program
40–59	3	7	8	11			4	3	1	7	2	4	in
20–39	3	5	5	9			2	2	1	5	4	3	1951
0–19	1	2	3	5			2	1		2	1		
Number of Students Ranked	48	35	46	46			19	12	27	35	24	18	

1951 GROUP · JUNIOR YEAR

PERCENTILE RANK IN CLASS	CHICAGO S	C	COLUMBIA S	C	FISK S	C	GOUCHER S	C	LAFAYETTE S	C	LOUISVILLE S	C	MOREHOUSE S C
80–99	20	6	15	9	5	4	7	2	9	16	No data		Not in
60–79	12	5	12	6	4	5	2	4	5	8	reported		program
40–59	7	6	7	7	2	3	2		5	1			in
20–39	1	8	6	5	1	6	1	1	2	5			1951
0–19	4	3	3	6	2	5			2	3			
Number of Students Ranked	44	28	43	33	14	23	12	7	23	33			

1951 GROUP · SENIOR YEAR

PERCENTILE RANK IN CLASS	CHICAGO S	C	COLUMBIA S	C	FISK S	C	GOUCHER S	C	LAFAYETTE S	C	LOUISVILLE S	C	MOREHOUSE S C
80–99	*		17	6	1	4	7	2	7	14	3	5	Not in
60–79			6	9		7	2	3	6	8	6	5	program
40–59			6	3	1	6	2	2	7	3	1	2	in
20–39			2	4		2	1		1	3			1951
0–19			4	4		3		1		5			
Number of Students Ranked			35	26	2	22	12	8	21	33	10	12	

* No formal class structure and no ranking system for graduating students.
** Ranking not comparable because of special academic programs for Scholars.

TABLE V

ACADEMIC PERFORMANCE OF SCHOLARS
AND COMPARISON STUDENTS

A. *Percentile Rank in Class*

1951 GROUP · FRESHMAN YEAR

OBERLIN		SHIMER		UTAH		WISCONSIN		YALE		TOTAL S NO.	%	C NO.	%
S	C	S	C	S	C	S	C	S	C				
6	10	5	†	10	11	28	12	17	16	117	41.2	85	31.5
7	5	5		9	15	7	6	10	16	61	21.5	75	27.8
6	6	4		11	9	3	5	7	7	56	19.7	44	16.3
2	7	6		4	14		4	9	6	35	12.3	49	18.1
	1	4			2		1	6	6	15	5.3	17	6.3
21	29	24		34	51	38	28	49	51	284		270	

1951 GROUP · SOPHOMORE YEAR

OBERLIN		SHIMER		UTAH		WISCONSIN		YALE		TOTAL S NO.	%	C NO.	%
S	C	S	C	S	C	S	C	S	C				
7	8	3		15	11	26	12	11	12	151	46.7	89	31.0
4	7	4		7	8	10	11	6	11	66	20.4	71	24.7
4	4	6		8	8		1	13	10	49	15.2	55	19.2
4	7	9		3	8		2	6	7	37	11.5	48	16.7
2	3	2			2	2	2	7	7	20	6.2	24	8.4
21	29	24		33	37	38	28	43	47	323		287	

1951 GROUP · JUNIOR YEAR

OBERLIN		SHIMER		UTAH		WISCONSIN		YALE		TOTAL S NO.	%	C NO.	%
S	C	S	C	S	C	S	C	S	C				
6	10	2		14	3	16	10	12	9	106	41.1	69	31.5
3	3	1		11	4	4	1	10	10	64	24.8	46	21.0
4	5	1		5	2	1	2	3	11	37	14.3	37	16.9
3	1	4		2	7		1	10	6	30	11.6	40	18.3
1	3	4			4		1	5	2	21	8.1	27	12.3
17	22	12		32	20	21	15	40	38	258		219	

1951 GROUP · SENIOR YEAR

OBERLIN		SHIMER		UTAH		WISCONSIN		YALE		TOTAL S NO.	%	C NO.	%
S	C	S	C	S	C	S	C	S	C				
3	9			No		17	9	16	11	71	41.3	60	32.3
7	2			data		4	4	12	12	43	25.0	50	26.9
1	4			reported		2	1	5	11	25	14.5	32	17.2
3	6	2				3	2	8	9	20	11.6	26	13.9
2	1	3				2	2	2	2	13	7.5	18	9.7
16	22	5				28	18	43	45	172		186	

† Shimer had no Comparison students.

TABLE V *continued*

ACADEMIC PERFORMANCE OF SCHOLARS
AND COMPARISON STUDENTS

A. *Percentile Rank in Class (continued)*

1952 GROUP · FRESHMAN YEAR

PERCENTILE RANK IN CLASS	CHICAGO S	CHICAGO C	COLUMBIA S	COLUMBIA C	FISK S	FISK C	GOUCHER S	GOUCHER C	LAFAYETTE S	LAFAYETTE C	LOUISVILLE S	LOUISVILLE C	MOREHOUSE S	MOREHOUSE C
80–99	25	17	17	12	*		9	10	9	12	14	9	15	7
60–79	10	12	10	12			7	6	4	8	4	5	5	9
40–59	9	7	8	8			5	8	5	4	1	1	2	9
20–39	5	6	6	10				1	1	3	4	4	4	1
0–19	2	3	5	9				1	2	2		2	1	3
Number of Students Ranked	51	45	46	51			21	26	21	29	23	21	27	29

1952 GROUP · SOPHOMORE YEAR

PERCENTILE RANK IN CLASS	CHICAGO S	CHICAGO C	COLUMBIA S	COLUMBIA C	FISK S	FISK C	GOUCHER S	GOUCHER C	LAFAYETTE S	LAFAYETTE C	LOUISVILLE S	LOUISVILLE C	MOREHOUSE S	MOREHOUSE C
80–99	23	16	21	10	10	12	10	12	11	8	No		16	6
60–79	8	7	8	8	5	3	8	4	2	7	data		2	4
40–59	9	6	4	6	6	1	2	3	3	8	reported		3	4
20–39	7	2	5	12	2	6		2	1	3				
0–19	2	1	7	7	4	4		1						1
Number of Students Ranked	49	32	45	43	27	26	20	22	17	26			21	15

1952 GROUP · JUNIOR YEAR

PERCENTILE RANK IN CLASS	CHICAGO S	CHICAGO C	COLUMBIA S	COLUMBIA C	FISK S	FISK C	GOUCHER S	GOUCHER C	LAFAYETTE S	LAFAYETTE C	LOUISVILLE S	LOUISVILLE C	MOREHOUSE S	MOREHOUSE C
80–99	11	5	14	9	2	10	9	6	10	9	4	2	7	3
60–79	7	1	10	8	5	3	3	5	3	6	5	7	8	9
40–59	9	2	6	7	2	3	5	5	1	5	3	6	2	
20–39	1	4	6	5	4	5		2	1	3				
0–19	4	1	5	9	5	2		1		2	1			
Number of Students Ranked	32	13	41	38	18	23	17	19	15	25	13	15	17	12

1952 GROUP · SENIOR YEAR

PERCENTILE RANK IN CLASS	CHICAGO S	CHICAGO C	COLUMBIA S	COLUMBIA C	FISK S	FISK C	GOUCHER S	GOUCHER C	LAFAYETTE S	LAFAYETTE C	LOUISVILLE S	LOUISVILLE C	MOREHOUSE S	MOREHOUSE C
80–99	**		11	9	5	7	10	7	10	8	5	1	8	4
60–79			13	2	2	3	4	7	3	3	1		5	4
40–59			2	7	1	2	3	5		6		1	2	1
20–39			4	3	1	3		1	1	3	2	1	1	1
0–19			8	9	1	2			1	2		1	1	1
Number of Students Ranked			38	30	10	17	17	20	15	22	8	4	17	11

* Ranking not comparable because of special academic programs for Scholars.

** No ranking system for graduating students.

TABLE V *continued*

ACADEMIC PERFORMANCE OF SCHOLARS
AND COMPARISON STUDENTS

A. *Percentile Rank in Class (continued)*

1952 GROUP • FRESHMAN YEAR

OBERLIN		SHIMER		UTAH		WISCONSIN		YALE		TOTAL S		C	
s	c	s	c	s	c	s	c	s	c	NO.	%	NO.	%
8	13	8	†	21	19	25	15	13	19	164	43.6	133	33.6
6	15	9		14	17	6	8	10	16	85	22.6	108	27.3
7	7	4		7	12	1	3	8	11	57	15.2	70	17.7
2	3	4		1	10	4	5	10	6	41	10.9	49	12.4
5	1	7		1	5	1	4	5	6	29	7.7	36	9.0
28	39	32		44	63	37	35	46	58	376		396	

1952 GROUP • SOPHOMORE YEAR

OBERLIN		SHIMER		UTAH		WISCONSIN		YALE		TOTAL S		C	
s	c	s	c	s	c	s	c	s	c	NO.	%	NO.	%
7	12	7		19	2	24	9	5	15	153	44.5	102	36.8
6	8	3		12	4	3	7	7	14	64	18.6	66	23.8
4	5	5		6		3	4	9	9	54	15.7	46	16.6
1	5	5		4	2	1	2	15	8	41	11.9	42	15.2
3	1	4		2		1	1	9	5	32	9.3	21	7.6
21	31	24		43	8	32	23	45	51	344		277	

1952 GROUP • JUNIOR YEAR

OBERLIN		SHIMER		UTAH		WISCONSIN		YALE		TOTAL S		C	
s	c	s	c	s	c	s	c	s	c	NO.	%	NO.	%
3	8	1		20	15	20	4	8	21	109	38.0	92	33.5
7	9	3		11	5	6	3	5	11	73	25.4	67	24.4
3	6	1		6	5		2	4	10	42	14.6	51	18.5
7	2	1			2	3	4	10	4	33	11.5	31	11.3
4	3	1		1	5	2	2	7	9	30	10.5	34	12.3
24	28	7		38	32	31	15	34	55	287		275	

1952 GROUP • SENIOR YEAR

OBERLIN		SHIMER		UTAH		WISCONSIN		YALE		TOTAL S		C	
s	c	s	c	s	c	s	c	s	c	NO.	%	NO.	%
3	12			13	9	21	7	5	15	91	43.8	79	36.7
7	5			5	8	5	7	6	10	51	24.5	49	22.8
3	6	1		1	2		3	7	4	20	9.6	37	17.2
1	4	1		3	4	2	4	8	6	24	11.5	30	14.0
4	1	1		2		2		4	2	22	10.5	20	9.3
18	28	3		22	25	30	21	30	37	208		215	

† Shimer had no Comparison students.

TABLE V *continued*

ACADEMIC PERFORMANCE OF SCHOLARS
AND COMPARISON STUDENTS

A. *Percentile Rank in Class (continued)*

1953 GROUP • FRESHMAN YEAR

PERCENTILE RANK IN CLASS	CHICAGO S	C	COLUMBIA S	C	FISK S	C	GOUCHER S	C	LAFAYETTE S	C	LOUISVILLE S	C	MOREHOUSE S	C
80–99	13	10	11	8	12	6	10	9	8	8	No		18	11
60–79	4	6	3	5	8	6	3	4	1	2	data		5	9
40–59	3	2	2	5	5	6			3	5	reported		1	8
20–39	2	2	5	2	2	6	2	2	1	2			1	4
0–19	1	2	3	2	2	4				1			2	2
Number of Students Ranked	23	22	24	22	29	28	15	15	13	18			27	34

1953 GROUP • SOPHOMORE YEAR

	CHICAGO S	C	COLUMBIA S	C	FISK S	C	GOUCHER S	C	LAFAYETTE S	C	LOUISVILLE S	C	MOREHOUSE S	C
80–99	11	8	8	6	13	10	9	8	8	7	2	6	10	8
60–79	3	3	4	4	6	4	3	4	2	2	11	8	10	7
40–59	3	4	4	4	5	3	1	1	2	2	6	3	2	4
20–39	1	1	4	6	1	2	2		1	4				1
0–19		3	3	1		2		2	1	2				
Number of Students Ranked	18	19	23	21	25	21	15	15	14	17	19	17	22	20

1954 GROUP • FRESHMAN YEAR

	CHICAGO S	C	COLUMBIA S	C	FISK S	C	GOUCHER S	C	LAFAYETTE S	C	LOUISVILLE S	C	MOREHOUSE S	C
80–99	10	6	11	4	13	6	9	11	No new		1	2	11	3
60–79	3	3	5	5	10	7	4	1	groups in		9	12	7	15
40–59	3	5	3	7	1	7	2	5	program		8	4	5	6
20–39	2	2	1	4	1	2			in		1	1	1	
0–19		3	2	2	2	1	2		1954					
Number of Students Ranked	18	19	22	22	27	23	17	17			19	19	24	24

ACADEMIC PERFORMANCE OF SCHOLARS
AND COMPARISON STUDENTS

A. *Percentile Rank in Class (continued)*

1953 GROUP · FRESHMAN YEAR

OBERLIN		SHIMER		UTAH		WISCONSIN		YALE		TOTAL S NO.	S %	C NO.	C %
S	C	S	C	S	C	S	C	S	C				
9	9	6	†	17	13	7	13	3		114	49.8	87	40.1
4	6	5		7	9	1	3	1	No data reported	42	18.3	50	23.0
1	3	10		5	3	5				35	15.3	32	14.7
2	4	5		6	6		1			26	11.4	29	13.4
1	1	1		2	7					12	5.2	19	8.8
17	23	27		37	38	13	17	4		229		217	

1953 GROUP · SOPHOMORE YEAR

OBERLIN		SHIMER	UTAH		WISCONSIN		YALE		TOTAL S NO.	S %	C NO.	C %
7	8	8	18	12	6	12	2	7	102	43.4	91	43.5
6	7	9	5	8	1	2	5	3	65	27.7	52	24.9
	4	6	8	4				3	37	15.7	32	15.3
3	3	4		2	1	2	1	3	18	7.7	24	11.5
1		3			4		1		13	5.5	10	4.8
17	22	30	31	26	12	16	9	15	235		209	

1954 GROUP · FRESHMAN YEAR

OBERLIN		SHIMER	UTAH		WISCONSIN		YALE		TOTAL S NO.	S %	C NO.	C %
5	6	10	25	15	10	15	1		106	47.5	68	34.7
4	4	4	3	9	3	3		No Comparison students	52	23.3	59	30.1
2	3	5		2	2	2	1		32	14.3	41	20.9
2	4	7	2		3	4	1		21	9.4	17	8.7
3	4	3				1			12	5.4	11	5.6
16	21	29	30	26	18	25	3		223		196	

† Shimer had no Comparison students.

TABLE V *continued*

ACADEMIC PERFORMANCE OF SCHOLARS
AND COMPARISON STUDENTS

B. *Academic Standing of Scholars Related to Number of Years of Schooling Completed*

YEARS OF SCHOOLING COMPLETED:	FRESHMAN YEAR			SOPHOMORE YEAR			JUNIOR YEAR			SENIOR YEAR		
	10–10½	11–11½	12	10–10½	11–11½	12	10–10½	11–11½	12	10–10½	11–11½	12
						1951 GROUP						
PERCENTILE RANK IN CLASS												
80–99	36.6	46.4	29.6	43.6	50.0	40.7	36.6	47.0	28.0	33.9	45.5	*
60–79	21.1	19.0	37.0	20.6	20.0	22.2	18.8	26.5	40.0	26.2	22.7	
40–59	19.2	20.3	18.5	15.9	13.0	25.9	14.8	13.6	16.0	13.8	16.0	
20–39	12.5	13.1	7.4	11.9	11.8	7.4	15.8	7.6	16.0	13.9	10.2	
0–19	10.6	1.3	7.4	8.0	5.3	3.7	13.9	5.3	0.0	12.3	5.7	
Number of Scholars Rated	104	153	27	126	170	27	101	132	25	65	88	18
						1952 GROUP						
80–99	42.8	47.6	33.3	44.6	42.9	53.7	39.6	36.6	38.2	51.5	38.5	29.4
60–79	21.1	22.3	26.2	18.0	19.1	12.2	20.7	27.5	32.4	19.1	26.9	38.2
40–59	13.8	15.0	21.4	18.7	14.8	7.3	14.9	16.8	5.9	10.3	12.8	2.9
20–39	12.6	9.6	9.6	11.0	13.3	12.2	11.6	9.9	17.7	8.8	10.3	17.6
0–19	9.6	5.4	9.5	7.8	9.8	14.6	13.3	9.1	5.9	10.3	11.5	11.8
Number of Scholars Rated	166	166	42	155	142	41	121	131	34	68	78	34

* Number of cases judged too small for computing percentages.

ACADEMIC PERFORMANCE OF SCHOLARS

AND COMPARISON STUDENTS

B. *Academic Standing of Scholars Related to Number*
of Years of Schooling Completed (continued)

YEARS OF SCHOOLING COMPLETED:	FRESHMAN YEAR			SOPHOMORE YEAR			JUNIOR YEAR			SENIOR YEAR		
	10– 10½	11– 11½	12	10– 10½	11– 11½	12	10– 10½	11– 11½	12	10– 10½	11– 11½	12
					1953 GROUP							
PERCENTILE RANK IN CLASS												
80–99	48.2	51.7	*	45.4	52.9	*						
60–79	15.6	20.4		26.7	19.2							
40–59	20.5	12.7		13.3	17.4							
20–39	10.8	11.0		9.3	5.8							
0–19	4.8	4.2		5.3	4.8							
Number of Scholars Rated	83	118	22	75	104	19						
					1954 GROUP							
80–99	40.8	51.9	*									
60–79	23.5	24.1										
40–59	14.8	13.1										
20–39	13.6	7.4										
0–19	7.4	3.6										
Number of Scholars Rated	81	137	4									

* Number of cases judged too small for computing percentages.

TABLE V *continued*

ACADEMIC PERFORMANCE OF SCHOLARS
AND COMPARISON STUDENTS

C. *Mean Scaled Scores of Scholars and Comparison Students*
on Area Tests of the Graduate Record Examinations

GROUP	CHICAGO		COLUMBIA		FISK		GOUCHER		LAFAYETTE		LOUISVILLE		MOREHOUSE	
	S	C	S	C	S	C	S	C	S	C	S	C	S	C
1952 Group as Sophomores														
Social Science	606	613	590	580	436	404	593	570	498	490	506	477	462	376
Humanities	635	643	614	599	457	467	671	625	482	464	497	427	488	431
Natural Science	646	687	639	637	438	444	595	576	590	578	540	485	518	462
1953 Group as Sophomores														
Social Science	593	632	582	603	355	345	571	534	536	535	494	494	411	388
Humanities	676	654	639	612	438	403	622	599	541	546	510	452	451	421
Natural Science	605	635	607	586	416	402	559	535	574	578	509	485	456	445
1954 Group as Sophomores														
Social Science	602	562	609	574	382	356	604	579	No Scholars or Comparison Students in 1954		423	414	420	366
Humanities	685	614	635	591	440	414	652	646			470	439	455	405
Natural Science	655	576	638	617	426	438	595	557			522	535	480	451
1951 Group as Seniors														
Social Science	664	658	641	651	441	422	603	602	550	521	505	510	Not in program in 1951	
Humanities	723	676	673	672	429	439	654	658	529	519	522	519		
Natural Science	676	669	611	625	466	452	579	507	561	574	525	500		
1952 Group as Seniors														
Social Science	656	641	649	641	495	441	633	577	573	538	592	490	514	419
Humanities	711	688	671	636	492	455	715	648	525	509	605	545	495	410
Natural Science	691	699	665	624	455	419	612	589	647	608	630	610	564	446

Number of students tested:	SCHOLARS	COMPARISONS
1952 Sophomores	358	292
1953 Sophomores	187	158
1954 Sophomores	186	127
1951 Seniors	192	144
1952 Seniors	226	157
TOTAL	1,149	878

TABLE V *continued*

ACADEMIC PERFORMANCE OF SCHOLARS
AND COMPARISON STUDENTS

C. *Mean Scaled Scores of Scholars and Comparison Students*
on Area Tests of the Graduate Record Examinations

OBERLIN		SHIMER		UTAH		WISCONSIN		YALE		MEAN SCORES OF TOTAL GROUP		TEST NORMS
S	C	S	C	S	C	S	C	S	C	S	C	
												For other Sophomores, 1954:
569	571	552	‡	529	506	599	572	601	574	558	527	430
596	610	607		522	494	568	518	623	571	575	540	458
626	593	581		585	555	658	609	613	615	598	576	455
												For other Sophomores, 1955:
587	555	539		535	475	543	593	†	*	512	504	405
624	593	626		522	494	579	591	†	*	550	529	450
609	564	562		559	545	558	591	†	*	539	529	445
												For other Sophomores, 1956:
553	578	573		517	472	565	569	*	*	523	488	389
621	589	578		572	544	554	542	*	*	564	525	431
598	584	582		599	546	603	611	*	*	569	537	452
												For other Seniors, 1955:
618	579	506		568	493	666	589	657	635	620	557	444
641	656	664		609	560	639	600	636	637	632	578	460
598	569	526		603	499	667	605	585	577	606	558	452
												For other Seniors, 1956:
624	623	540		580	617	640	617	635	611	608	579	438
678	687	660		559	569	636	607	671	624	630	600	464
654	628	590		632	601	685	612	651	618	632	591	459

‡ No comparison students.
† Number of students insufficient to provide distribution.
* Not tested.

TABLE VI

ADJUSTMENT OF THE SCHOLARS AND COMPARISON STUDENTS

A. *Faculty Ratings on Over-all Adjustment*

1951 GROUP AS FRESHMEN

RATING	CHICAGO s	c	COLUMBIA s	c	FISK s	c	GOUCHER s	c	LAFAYETTE s	c	LOUISVILLE s	c	MOREHOUSE s	c
Excellent	6	11	15	4	8	5	4	3	3	6	2	2	Not in	
Good	20	15	16	24	14	16	4	6	11	16	2	3	program	
Moderately Good	17	5	12	15	3	4	9	1	10	13	2		in	
Poor	4	4	4	3	2		2	2	3				1951	
Very Poor	1													
Number of Students Rated	48	35	47	46	27	25	19	12	27	35	6	5		

1952 GROUP AS FRESHMEN

RATING	CHICAGO s	c	COLUMBIA s	c	FISK s	c	GOUCHER s	c	LAFAYETTE s	c	LOUISVILLE s	c	MOREHOUSE s	c
Excellent	8	9	4	5	11	3		3	1	1	1	1		2
Good	23	18	26	23	12	16	10	16	8	13	1	1	17	19
Moderately Good	12	16	14	19	11	8	11	5	9	13	2	3	7	6
Poor	8	3	1	4	1	2		2	3	2	3		3	2
Very Poor		1	1		1									
Number of Students Rated	51	47	46	51	36	29	21	26	21	29	7	5	27	29

1953 GROUP AS FRESHMEN

RATING	CHICAGO s	c	COLUMBIA s	c	FISK s	c	GOUCHER s	c	LAFAYETTE s	c	LOUISVILLE s	c	MOREHOUSE s	c
Excellent	3	3	1	1	4	3			5	4			3	2
Good	12	14	16	12	17	17	7	6	6	12			15	23
Moderately Good	5	4	4	7	5	5	6	9	2	2	No data		9	9
Poor	1		1	3	3	1	1				reported			
Very Poor	2		2				1							
Number of Students Rated	23	21	24	23	29	26	15	15	13	18			27	34

1954 GROUP AS FRESHMEN

RATING	CHICAGO s	c	COLUMBIA s	c	FISK s	c	GOUCHER s	c	LAFAYETTE s	c	LOUISVILLE s	c	MOREHOUSE s	c
Excellent	7	2	7	3	8	3	1		No new					
Good	6	10	10	11	14	9	7	6	groups		18	18	21	22
Moderately Good	5	7	3	7	2	6	7	10	in			1	3	3
Poor		1	2		2	2	2	1	program		1			
Very Poor	1			1	1									
Number of Students Rated	19	20	22	22	27	20	17	17			19	19	24	25

ADJUSTMENT OF THE SCHOLARS AND COMPARISON STUDENTS

A. *Faculty Ratings on Over-all Adjustment*

1951 GROUP AS FRESHMEN

OBERLIN s	OBERLIN c	SHIMER s	SHIMER c	UTAH s	UTAH c	WISCONSIN s	WISCONSIN c	YALE s	YALE c	TOTAL S NO.	TOTAL S %	TOTAL C NO.	TOTAL C %
3	7	10	*	7	**	14	**	8	14	80	23.4	52	21.7
5	10	7		18		15		21	18	133	38.9	108	45.4
10	10	4		5		7		10	13	89	26.0	61	25.4
3	2	3		3		2		9	6	35	10.2	17	7.1
								4	1	5	1.5	1	.4
21	29	24		33		38		52	52	342		239	

1952 GROUP AS FRESHMEN

OBERLIN s	OBERLIN c	SHIMER s	SHIMER c	UTAH s	UTAH c	WISCONSIN s	WISCONSIN c	YALE s	YALE c	TOTAL S NO.	TOTAL S %	TOTAL C NO.	TOTAL C %
4	8	7		8	**	7	**	9	20	60	15.3	52	16.6
9	19	12		22		20		20	24	180	45.8	149	47.5
9	8	10		9		9		14	12	117	29.8	90	28.7
2	4	3		2				4	3	30	7.6	22	7.0
3				1						6	1.5	1	.3
27	39	32		42		36		47	59	393		314	

1953 GROUP AS FRESHMEN

OBERLIN s	OBERLIN c	SHIMER s	SHIMER c	UTAH s	UTAH c	WISCONSIN s	WISCONSIN c	YALE s	YALE c	TOTAL S NO.	TOTAL S %	TOTAL C NO.	TOTAL C %
2	7	13		1	**	3	**	1	**	36	15.7	20	12.5
4	12	10		27		6		1		121	52.8	96	60.0
9	4	4		6		2		2		54	23.6	40	25.0
2				3		2				13	5.7	4	2.5
										5	2.2	0	0
17	23	27		37		13		4		229		160	

1954 GROUP AS FRESHMEN

OBERLIN s	OBERLIN c	SHIMER s	SHIMER c	UTAH s	UTAH c	WISCONSIN s	WISCONSIN c	YALE s	YALE c	TOTAL S NO.	TOTAL S %	TOTAL C NO.	TOTAL C %
3	8	8		2	**	4	**		**	40	17.9	16	11.1
5	8	9		26		8		1		125	55.8	84	58.3
6	5	8		1		6		1		42	18.8	39	27.1
2		4		1				1		15	6.7	4	2.8
										2	.9	1	.7
16	21	29		30		18		3		224		144	

* Shimer had no Comparison students.
** No data available.

TABLE VI *continued*

A. *Faculty Ratings on Over-all Adjustments (continued)*

1951 GROUP AS SENIORS

RATING	CHICAGO		COLUMBIA		FISK		GOUCHER		LAFAYETTE		LOUISVILLE		MOREHOUSE	
	S	C	S	C	S	C	S	C	S	C	S	C	S	C
Excellent	10	2	13	8	2	10	3	2	2	9	2	3	Not	
Good	14	9	15	15	2	8	4	5	15	20	10	9	in	
Moderately Good	5	6	12	8	1	2	5	1	3	4			program	
Poor	1	2	2	4					1				in	
Very Poor		1		3									1951	
Number of Students Rated	30	20	42	38	5	20	12	8	21	33	12	12		

1952 GROUP AS SENIORS

	CHICAGO		COLUMBIA		FISK		GOUCHER		LAFAYETTE		LOUISVILLE		MOREHOUSE	
Excellent	3		9	10	7	6	5	2	4	9	1	3	3	1
Good	11	14	20	18	6	8	9	14	11	14	5	8	6	9
Moderately Good	6	3	9	9	4		3	4			6	6	9	1
Poor	4	1	1	1	1	2					1	1	1	
Very Poor	1			2										
Number of Students Rated	25	18	39	40	18	16	17	20	15	23	13	18	19	11

B. *Faculty and Administrative Opinion as to Wisdom of Early Admission as Expressed at End of Senior Year*

1951 SCHOLARS

OPINION	CHICAGO		COLUMBIA		FISK		GOUCHER		LAFAYETTE		LOUISVILLE		MOREHOUSE	
	NO.	%	NO.	%	NO.	%	NO.	%	NO.	%	NO.	%	NO.	%
Wise	26	89.7	34	77.3	10	100.0	10	83.3	18	85.7	9	75.0	Not in	
Opinion Divided	2	6.9	6	13.6			2	16.7	2	9.5	3	25.0	program	
Unwise	1	3.4	4	9.1					1	4.8			in 1951	
Number of Scholars Rated	29		44		10		12		21		12			

1952 SCHOLARS

	CHICAGO		COLUMBIA		FISK		GOUCHER		LAFAYETTE		LOUISVILLE		MOREHOUSE	
Wise	24	80.0	29	74.4	17	81.0	16	94.1	13	81.3	8	61.5	18	94.7
Opinion Divided	4	13.3	8	20.5	3	14.3	1	5.9	2	12.5	5	38.5	1	5.3
Unwise	2	6.7	2	5.1	1	4.7			1	6.3				
Number of Scholars Rated	30		39		21		17		16		13		19	

T A B L E   V I *continued*

A. *Faculty Ratings on Over-all Adjustments (continued)*

1951 GROUP AS SENIORS

OBERLIN s	OBERLIN c	SHIMER s	SHIMER c	UTAH s	UTAH c	WISCONSIN s	WISCONSIN c	YALE s	YALE c	TOTAL s NO.	TOTAL s %	TOTAL c NO.	TOTAL c %
1	2	3	*	4	**	12	**	8	16	60	23.6	52	26.4
5	5	1		24		10		18	15	118	46.5	86	43.7
9	14	1		10		5		7	11	58	22.8	46	23.4
2	1					1		6	2	13	5.1	9	4.6
1								4		5	2.0	4	2.0
18	22	5		38		28		43	44	254		197	

1952 GROUP AS SENIORS

OBERLIN s	OBERLIN c	SHIMER s	SHIMER c	UTAH s	UTAH c	WISCONSIN s	WISCONSIN c	YALE s	YALE c	TOTAL s NO.	TOTAL s %	TOTAL c NO.	TOTAL c %
3	3	1		8	**	9	9	2	10	55	20.6	53	20.5
10	15			14		20	21	13	32	125	46.8	153	59.3
6	9	1		4		4	2	17	9	69	25.8	43	16.7
1	1	1		1		2		3	1	16	6.0	7	2.7
				1						2	.7	2	.8
20	28	3		28		35	32	35	52	267		258	

B. *Faculty and Administrative Opinion as to Wisdom of Early Admission as Expressed at End of Senior Year*

1951 SCHOLARS

OBERLIN NO.	OBERLIN %	SHIMER NO.	SHIMER %	UTAH NO.	UTAH %	WISCONSIN NO.	WISCONSIN %	YALE NO.	YALE %	TOTAL NO.	TOTAL %
10	55.6	5	100.0	37	97.4	24	82.8	24	57.1	207	79.6
6	33.3			1	2.6	4	13.8	12	28.6	38	14.6
2	11.1					1	3.4	6	14.3	15	5.8
18		5		38		29		42		260	

1952 SCHOLARS

OBERLIN NO.	OBERLIN %	SHIMER NO.	SHIMER %	UTAH NO.	UTAH %	WISCONSIN NO.	WISCONSIN %	YALE NO.	YALE %	TOTAL NO.	TOTAL %
19	90.5	2	66.7	30	83.3	30	81.1	17	42.5	223	76.4
1	4.8	1	33.3	1	2.8	5	13.5	18	45.0	50	17.1
1	4.8			5	13.9	2	5.4	5	12.5	19	6.5
21		3		36		37		40		292	

* Shimer had no Comparison students.
** No data reported.

TABLE VI *continued*

C. *Failures, Withdrawals, and Transfers*

1951 GROUP

| | FAILURES | | | | | | WITHDRAWALS FOR REASONS OTHER THAN FAILURE | | | | | |
| | SCHOLARS | | COMPARS. | | CLASSMATES* | | SCHOLARS | | COMPARS. | | CLASSMATES* | |
COLLEGE	NO.	%	NO.	%	NO.	%	NO.	%	NO.	%	NO.	%
CHICAGO	7	11.6	8	14.0			3	5.0	8	14.0		
COLUMBIA	8	15.7	2	4.4	—	—	1	2.0	8	17.4	—	—
FISK	4	14.3	1	3.6			4	14.3	1	3.6		
GOUCHER	1	5.3	2	10.6	8	7.0	3	15.8	3	15.8	29	25.2
LAFAYETTE	4	13.4	4	10.0	90	26	1	3.3	0	0.0	21	6
LOUISVILLE	2	6.9	0	0.0	—	6	6	20.7	8	33.3	—	17
MOREHOUSE	Not in Program in 1951											
OBERLIN	2	8.0	2	6.7	59	15	2	8.0	3	10.0	18	6
SHIMER	3	8.8	No Comps.		5	10.6	7	20.6	No Comps.		5	10.6
UTAH	0	0.0	3	5.7	—	—	19	47.5	16	30.8	—	—
WISCONSIN	6	11.5	8	11.8			2	3.8	13	19.1		
YALE	10	19.2	4	7.8	99	9.2	0	0.0	2	3.9	91	8.5
1951 *Total*	47	11.2	34	8.2			48	11.4	62	14.9		

1952 GROUP

CHICAGO	8	14.8	7	13.0			1	1.9	5	9.3		
COLUMBIA	0	0.0	1	2.3	—	—	1	2.2	3	6.8	—	—
FISK	5	13.9	0	0.0			6	16.7	5	16.7		
GOUCHER	0	0.0	0	0.0	4	3.7	2	9.1	3	11.1	21	19.3
LAFAYETTE	4	17.3	3	10.3	124	29	2	8.7	2	6.9	37	8
LOUISVILLE	10	34.5	4	15.4	—	6	4	13.8	6	23.1	—	17
MOREHOUSE	6	20.7	6	17.2			2	6.9	7	20.0		
OBERLIN	4	13.7	2	5.4	50	15	4	13.8	3	8.1	18	6
SHIMER	2	6.2	No Comps.		8	21.6	5	15.6	No Comps.		4	10.8
UTAH	5	11.1	10	12.5	—	—	7	15.6	26	32.5	—	—
WISCONSIN	5	10.5	9	17.3			3	6.3	2	3.8		
YALE	6	12.7	4	6.8	89	9.7	1	2.1	2	3.4	66	7.2
1952 *Total*	55	12.5	46	9.8			38	8.6	64	13.6		
Combined *Total*	102	11.9	80	9.0			86	10.0	126	14.2		

* A dash (—) indicates an incomplete breakdown of the total figure.

C. *Failures, Withdrawals, and Transfers*

1951 GROUP

	TRANSFERS						TOTAL ATTRITION					
	SCHOLARS		COMPARS.		CLASSMATES		SCHOLARS		COMPARS.		CLASSMATES	
COLLEGE	NO.	%	NO.	%	NO.	%	NO.	%	NO.	%	NO.	%
CHICAGO	3	5.0	5	8.7			13	21.7	21	36.8		
COLUMBIA	0	0.0	1	2.2	—	—	9	17.6	11	23.9	—	16*
FISK	10	35.7	1	3.6			18	64.3	3	10.7		
GOUCHER	3	15.8	3	15.8	15	13.0	7	36.8	8	42.1	52	45.2
LAFAYETTE	3	10.0	2	5.0	16	5	8	26.7	6	15.0	127	37
LOUISVILLE	6	20.7	0	0.0	—	11	14	48.3	8	33.3	—	34*
MOREHOUSE	Not in Program in 1951											
OBERLIN	6	24.0	3	10.0	93	24	10	40.0	8	26.7	170	45
SHIMER	12	35.3	No Comps.		15	31.9	22	64.7	No Comps.		25	53.2
UTAH	5	12.5	9	17.3	—	—	24	60.0	28	53.8	—	75*
WISCONSIN	15	28.8	0	0.0			23	44.2	21	30.9		
YALE	1	1.9	0	0.0	20	1.9	11	21.2	6	11.8	210	19.7
1951 *Total*	64	15.2	24	5.8			159	37.8	120	28.9		

1952 GROUP

CHICAGO	4	7.4	3	5.6			13	24.1	15	27.8		
COLUMBIA	1	2.2	0	0.0	—	—	2	4.3	4	9.1	—	16*
FISK	1	2.8	2	6.7			12	33.3	7	23.3		
GOUCHER	3	13.6	3	11.1	21	19.3	5	22.7	6	22.2	46	42.3
LAFAYETTE	1	4.3	0	0.0	13	3	7	30.4	5	17.2	174	40
LOUISVILLE	3	10.3	0	0.0	—	11	17	58.6	10	38.5	—	34*
MOREHOUSE	6	20.7	10	28.6			14	48.3	23	65.7		
OBERLIN	3	10.3	5	13.5	43	13	11	37.9	10	27.0	111	34
SHIMER	18	56.3	No Comps.		14	37.8	25	78.1	No Comps.		26	70.3
UTAH	4	8.9	4	5.0	—	—	16	35.6	40	50.0	—	75*
WISCONSIN	6	12.5	1	1.9			14	29.2	12	23.1		
YALE	2	4.3	1	1.7	14	1.5	9	19.1	7	12.1	169	18.4
1952 *Total*	52	11.8	29	6.1			145	32.9	139	29.5		
Combined *Total*	116	13.5	53	6.0			304	35.3	259	29.2		

* Estimated by college.

TABLE VII

PLANS FOR GRADUATE STUDY

PLANS FOR GRADUATE STUDY	CHICAGO		COLUMBIA		FISK		GOUCHER		LAFAYETTE		LOUISVILLE		MOREHOUSE	
	S	C	S	C	S	C	S	C	S	C	S	C	S	C
1951 GROUP														
Already In	23	17	4	4							2	3	Not in	
Yes	6	3	29	19	5	7	3	2	13	10	1	4	program	
After Military Service			1										in	
After Earning Money			1		3	10	6						1951	
No		1	3	5		1	3	4	6	23	8	1		
No data	18	15	4	7	2	7		5	3	1	4	8		
Total	47	36	42	35	10	25	12	11	22	34	15	16		
1952 GROUP														
Already In	14	21	1	3							3	3		
Yes	17	12	35	26	15	10	13	7	9	7	5	4	13	10
After Military Service				1						2		1		
After Earning Money		1			5	6	2	3					1	
No	3	2	2	3	1	2	2	10	6	14	5	9	3	2
No data	7	3	6	5	3	5		1	1	1				
Total	41	39	44	38	24	23	17	21	16	24	13	17	17	12

This table includes data only for those students who were continuing in school, were graduating, or were in graduate school as of the end of senior year.

TABLE VII

PLANS FOR GRADUATE STUDY

1951 GROUP

OBERLIN S	C	SHIMER S	C	UTAH S	C	WISCONSIN S	C	YALE S	C	TOTAL S NO.	%	C NO.	%
2			*	8	5	3	4	1	2	43	16.5	35	11.9
9	13	3		5	2	18		5	10	97	37.1	70	23.7
	2				2	1				2	.8	4	1.4
		2				1				13	5.0	10	3.4
5	7			4	8	1				30	11.5	50	16.9
		7			7	5	43	35	33	76	29.1	126	42.7
16	22	12		17	24	29	47	41	45	261		295	

1952 GROUP

OBERLIN S	C	SHIMER S	C	UTAH S	C	WISCONSIN S	C	YALE S	C	TOTAL S NO.	%	C NO.	%
			*	2	3	5	5		1	25	8.4	36	10.8
14	15	2		12	5	27	4	20	27	182	61.1	127	38.2
1	3			2	5	2	1	1	6	6	2.0	19	5.7
	2			4	1					12	4.0	13	3.9
3	8	1		7	14		16	15	16	48	16.1	96	28.8
			4	2	12		14	2	1	25	8.4	42	12.6
18	28	7		29	40	34	40	38	51	298		333	

* Shimer had no Comparison students.

TABLE VIII

INTENDED FIELD OF SPECIALIZATION
IN GRADUATE OR PROFESSIONAL SCHOOL

1951 GROUP

FIELD	CHICAGO S	CHICAGO C	COLUMBIA S	COLUMBIA C	FISK S	FISK C	GOUCHER S	GOUCHER C	LAFAYETTE S	LAFAYETTE C	LOUISVILLE S	LOUISVILLE C	MOREHOUSE S	MOREHOUSE C
Law	2	3	3	1			1		3	1	1			
Medicine	8	2	16	11	2	3	1		2	3	2	3		
Engineering			3						1					
Business	1	2	1	1		1	1	2		1			Not in	
Natural Sciences and Mathematics	11	7	5	1	2	1	1		2	2			program in	
Social Sciences	2	3	5	2	2	3	4		1	1			1951	
Humanities	2	1	1	3		4	1		4	2				
Education			1	1	1	1						3		
Other	3	2		2	1	1						1		
No data	18	16	7	13	2	11	3	9	9	24	12	9		
Total	47	36	42	35	10	25	12	11	22	34	15	16		

1952 GROUP

FIELD	CHICAGO S	CHICAGO C	COLUMBIA S	COLUMBIA C	FISK S	FISK C	GOUCHER S	GOUCHER C	LAFAYETTE S	LAFAYETTE C	LOUISVILLE S	LOUISVILLE C	MOREHOUSE S	MOREHOUSE C
Law	2	2	8	4	2	4	1	1	3	1	1	2	3	1
Medicine	5	2	15	10	3			2	3	2	5	6	7	3
Engineering		1	4	5						1				
Business	1		1	3		1								2
Natural Sciences and Mathematics	8	15	5	3	6	2	4	3	1	2			3	
Social Sciences	9	4	1		7	4	3	2		1			1	2
Humanities	3	5		5	1	2	3	4	2		1			1
Education		2	1			2	1							1
Other				1	1									
No data	13	8	8	8	4	8	3	11	7	17	5	8	1	2
Total	41	39	44	38	24	23	17	21	16	24	12	16	15	12

This table includes those already in graduate school as of June, 1956, or who were then completing undergraduate work and had plans for graduate or professional school.

TABLE VIII

INTENDED FIELD OF SPECIALIZATION
IN GRADUATE OR PROFESSIONAL SCHOOL

1951 GROUP

| OBERLIN | | SHIMER | | UTAH | | WISCONSIN | | YALE | | TOTAL s | | c | |
s	c	s	c	s	c	s	c	s	c	NO.	%	NO.	%
			*	1	1	2	1	2	7	15	5.7	14	4.7
6	4			3	1	6	2	1	1	47	18.0	30	10.2
1		1			1			1		7	2.7	1	.3
				1	2				1	4	1.5	10	3.4
3				2	1	7				33	12.6	12	4.1
1	2					5			2	20	7.7	13	4.4
	4	1		3		1	1	1	1	14	5.4	16	5.4
	2	1		1	1					4	1.5	8	2.7
	2			2	1	2		1		9	3.4	9	3.1
4	8	9		3	16	6	43	35	33	108	41.4	182	61.7
15	22	12		16	24	29	47	41	45	261		295	

1952 GROUP

| OBERLIN | | SHIMER | | UTAH | | WISCONSIN | | YALE | | TOTAL s | | c | |
s	c	s	c	s	c	s	c	s	c	NO.	%	NO.	%
1			*	1	2	1	2	5	7	28	9.5	26	7.9
6	2	1		1	2	19	5	7	5	74	25.1	37	11.2
2				3	2			3	4	12	4.1	13	3.9
				1	2			1	1	4	1.4	9	2.7
3	7	1		7	1	7	1	2	3	47	15.9	37	11.2
2	2			1	3	4	1		1	28	9.5	20	6.0
1	6			4	2	3	1	2	7	20	6.7	33	10.0
	2			1				1		4	1.4	7	2.1
									1	2	.7	1	.3
3	8	5		10	26		30	17	22	76	25.7	148	44.7
18	27	7		29	40	34	40	38	51	295		331	

* Shimer had no Comparison students.